PEDALLING A DREAM

Ann Spencer

CCPS

Pedalling A Dream
First published in 2005 by:
Cwm Consultation and Publishing Service Ltd (CCPS),
Registered Office 2 Cwm Cottages, Ciltwrch,
Glasbury-on-Wye, Powys HR3 5NZ;
Company registered in Cardiff, Number 3690122,
© 2005 - Text, Ann Spencer
© 2005 - Illustrations, Michael Robinson

British Library Cataloguing in Publication Data
A catalogue record of this book is available from the
British Library ISBN 1-903235-03-0
Data base by key words: cycling, bicycle, fulfilling
dreams, aging, Lands End, John O Groats

Ilustrator: Michael Robinson
Editor: Phillipa May
Design and Printing co-ordinated by
Chapman and Chapman Associates & G. L. Print Ltd

CONTENTS PAGE

Dedicated to
Armchair Dreamers
Everywhere

ACKNOWLEGEMENTS

My grateful thanks, in no particular order, go to:

*My family and friends for their encouragement
and boundless enthusiasm*

The helpful strangers I met on the way

Bikewise of Ickenham for expert advice and excellent equipment

Phillipa May for telepathic editing

*Michael Robinson for making me laugh at myself
with his incomparable illustrations*

*Cwm Consultation and Publishing Service Ltd
for turning one adventure into two*

Dorothy and Barry Collins for their two-wheels wisdom

*And particularly my husband Will for not letting me
not do it in the first place.*

PREFACE

I have decided, at the age of 62, to cycle on my own from Land's End to John O'Groats.

The seed for this trip was planted long, long ago by Dervla Murphy's captivating account of her cycle ride from Dunkirk to Delhi, *Full Tilt*. I knew then that, at some point in my life on this planet, I would, like her, have to do a long ride of some sort. There were other books I read after that first one by women of various ages, all doing their cycling thing, some even going completely round the world for months, if not years, at a time. And they have all been inspirational.

I am a married woman, with two children and two grandchildren. I have had many jobs in my lifetime, but no career as such. My 'career' has been my family. But the dynamics of a woman's life change with the passing of time and the reshuffling of generations. These days, we are no longer expected to sit unheard and invisible in a corner knitting jumpers as soon as we hotch up a generation. So I think we need to take advantage of our longer life expectancy, widen our horizons and learn to become a little bit more of what others might call 'selfish'.

Then one day, I woke up thinking - I shall soon be too old to do anything *but* knit jumpers, my chance will have disappeared with time, our old enemy, and if I don't do it NOW, I never shall.

This book is written for all those people who, like me, would love to do something different, something out of their normal routine, something slightly daring, but who believe, for various reasons, that they ought not, should not, cannot, do it.

PART 1

CHAPTER 1 - Wheels in Motion

It was around the middle of July that I made my decision to do the trip, and immediately I started planning the route. From John O'Groats to Land's End! It's downhill, isn't it? And the weather, in late summer, is more likely to stay warm travelling from north to south. I thought I was being canny. I became terribly excited. Then I told my husband, Will, who also became excited. I told some cycling friends, Dot and Barry, and they became excited. But not before bursting my bubble of cleverness - they told me one cycles from south to north (prevailing wind, you see). Never mind about the warmth, one does not want to cycle 1000 miles into a head wind. I finally understood the wisdom of this first-hand on the one short stretch of the journey which found me cycling into the wind.

I think Dot and Barry were almost excited enough to come too, but in the end they settled for offering lots of good advice rather than company.

I joined both the Youth Hostel Association and the Cyclists' Touring Club, who between them have a selection of different routes for this classic ride – among them the scenic route, the B&B route, the fast route, the youth hostel route. In the event, the route I followed was the slow and steady if occasionally soggy one.

But there's only so much planning one can do in advance. After four weeks I have exhausted my interest in studying maps, plotting my overnight stops and piling up stuff to take in the corner of a room. I just want to be off and away and survive or die, so that I can get on with other things - before another idea possesses me!

Of course there have been other even more important things to organise besides staring at maps. Not having ridden a bicycle for years, other than short local forays as an occasional sop to keeping fit, and with only two rides of any significant length in my life, namely one 50-mile return trip from Bexhill-on-Sea to Camber Sands in my teens and a 30-mile ride on a long ago holiday with our children, I have been in dire need of practice.

Trips to the local supermarket have proved useful exercises in carrying stuff in my panniers, and a trial run to Slough where I have to catch the train to Cornwall and the start of my odyssey, was very enlightening. What should have been a relatively short (and easy) journey turned into a 30-mile round trip as I got lost on my way back, arriving home with jelly legs and the inescapable dread that this journey will take years, not months. But even so, I am becoming more confident on the bike all the time.

My bicycle, which I bought a few years ago, is a Ridgeback Metro Shimana Acera. Although it's just an ordinary general-purpose touring bike with derailleur gears, it does have, most importantly, a very comfortable saddle. It has also been fitted, for this trip, with new inner tyres as well as some very superior outer tyres. I'm hoping this will reduce the chance of punctures. The one lesson on puncture mending I have been given by Will has left me convinced that, if the need arises, I will just have to sit by the roadside and hope for a miracle - or try to look 21 and pretty. A miracle will be the most likely. But I suppose that if my life depends on it, I will manage, helped by my scribbled notes, to retrieve the lesson from my brain somewhere, and get the job done somehow. But I'm still baffled by how I'm going to find a bucket of water in the middle of nowhere!

I haven't needed to buy panniers as we already have two, but because they are so complicated to put on and take off, I just put them on and never take them off. Instead I have packed everything into plastic bags, which I will haul out, with as much dignity as I can muster, for my overnight stops. As I pack the panniers I'm reminded of 'My granny went shopping and in her panniers she put ...'. In my case, granny packed one waterproof jacket, one sports cardigan, one sports vest, two t-shirts, one pair of jogging trousers, one pair of shorts, two pairs of socks, two pairs of shoes, three sets of underwear, one scarf, one nightdress, one bag of toiletries, one towel and a baseball cap.

I have, though, bought a new small, efficient and beautifully designed pump, a mirror, some padded cycling gloves, and a pair of padded pants. Sore cycle bottoms are a thing of the past. And a tiny computer toy which tells me how many miles I cycle each day, the cumulative total, the time, the maximum speed, the minimum speed, the average speed - everything except the temperature in Timbuctoo and why I'm doing this!

Having grown up in an era when nobody wore a helmet, I have never worn one and, though I am not foolhardy, I decide not to now. It's not just me though. In cycling circles there is a good deal of controversy on the subject. Cycling organisations think the compulsory wearing of helmets could act as a deterrent in the battle being waged to get motorists out of their cars and onto their bikes, and it appears that not even the most ardent helmet wearers like the idea of people being made to wear them.

The weather has been wonderful for most of the summer so, rather than just sit on my idea for the winter, incubating my plans and brooding over them until spring, and then, more than likely, chickening out, it seems imperative to make a start here and now - set off for three weeks, see where I finish up, and start again from that spot next spring. And just hope that the weather holds! I am emphatically not a fair-weather-or-foul cyclist. Although I will reluctantly accept getting wet occasionally, I'm not prepared to be seriously cold or to struggle against wind. Or to camp! For one thing,

bad weather can be dangerous for cyclists, especially on main roads sharing space with thundering pantechnicons. But most importantly I want to enjoy myself, an ambitious goal when you think about the West Country hills!

CHAPTER 2 - Westward Ho!

So here I am, cycling to Slough! My main emotion - relief that I'm actually on my way after what seems an age of planning - is tinged with trepidation. The only pre-booking I have done is for the journey from Reading to Penzance and my first night at the youth hostel at St Just. After that I will be making it up as I go along, although I carry comprehensive lists of hostel and B&B accommodation along the route, provided by the YHA and CTC (Cycle Touring Club). Part of the reason for not doing much in the way of pre-booking, at least for the moment, is the sense of freedom that comes from not knowing in advance where I'll be laying my head on any one night. I like the open-endess of that concept - whether or not I shall like it in practice is another matter. My feelings as I set off, however, are mixed. Knowing that the success of my trip, my safety and my enjoyment are all down to me fills me with anxiety. On the other hand, I'm cycling in my own country for goodness sake, I speak the language and I have my mobile phone. All I have to do is put my feet on the pedals and turn the wheels.

I have been inordinately worried about the station at Slough and find it impossible to think about the journey beyond that point. So many potential problems run through my head that I believe it's highly likely that I will never manage to get both me and the bike safely onto the train. It makes John O'Groats an unimaginable destination.

Depending on which platform the train departs from for Reading, there's a possibility I shall have to somehow carry the bike up and down stairs, and my panniers are so heavy I can't actually lift the rear of the bike, however hard I have tried to pack light.

Initial enquries into timetabling and conditions at Slough Station have been met with, "don't know which platform that train will come into yet - too far ahead", and I cynically accept that they won't actually know until the train has been and gone!

As generally happens when an event has loomed so large, I discover that I have wasted considerable energy fretting. With two entrances to the station, both with wheelchair access to every platform, I encounter no problems reaching the right one for my train.

But the major anxiety has receded only for other, smaller ones to rush into the vacant space. I sit nervously waiting for the train to come, worrying about every little thing. Will I actually be able to get the bike onto the train? Will the train stop long enough for me to get on? Will it be the right one? Will it in fact stop at Reading? Will the train driver know the way? Worry, worry, worry.

Unsurprisingly, except perhaps to fellow worriers, everything goes according to plan and I eventually find myself on the Reading to Penzance train. I have not sat in my

reserved seat at the other end of the train, opting instead to occupy an unreserved one nearer to my bike. Not that I can see it of course, I just feel more comfortable knowing we are near each other!

The further away from London the train travels, the slower and more laborious its progress becomes, but also the more interesting from my cyclist's point of view. As we approach Devon and Cornwall I make a mental note of how hilly the landscape is around the many stations we stop at, so that I can make use of the new-found knowledge in the days to come to plot an achievable route.

It feels like the first time in many years that I have taken so much notice of where I am and what the landscape means to me. Branching out on my own is waking me up. It is the first time, I realise, that I have needed to pay such close attention. Will has always been with me before to plot routes and make decisions with – now I am seeing it all through just one pair of eyes.

By the time I get to Penzance, I'm dehydrated and can feel a headache threatening - in my anxiety, although I have drunk my coffee, I have forgotten to drink any water. But I forget all that as we arrive, dead on time, to a Penzance bathed in sunshine, making me feel all things are possible, and I retrieve my bike from the guard's van, ready to put my wheels in motion.

Penzance is a hilly little town but very pretty, and at the end of this especially glorious summer, still packed with holidaymakers. I ask a local shopkeeper the way to *San Joost* and am met with a completely blank stare. He asks to see the map and I point to St Just. Why have I pronounced it as a French name? It must be the heat. Or habit – perhaps it's because we have spent so many holidays in France that the mispronunciation is automatic.

He directs me at once, and I puff my way up and out of the main high street and find the right road to St Just. I continue puffing for the next seven miles, with very little time actually in the saddle. I am quickly learning that all roads in Cornwall go upwards. This is another very good reason for taking the south-north route – the Highlands of Scotland may sound more daunting, but there is nothing anywhere on the journey to compare with the Cornish hills.

After about an hour and a half of this exertion I am trembling with fatigue and stop for a muesli bar and water by the side of the road, feeling distinctly Dervla Murphy'ish. The view over the Cornish hills is stunning, with the late afternoon sunshine and warmth calming my rather ragged nerves. Eventually I arrive at the outskirts of St Just. Referring to the rough-and-ready map I have been sent by the hostel warden, I find it difficult to relate the squiggles to the present topography. While the sign to the YHA that I'm standing beside points $1\frac{1}{4}$ miles to the left, the

map seems to indicate that I need to go through the town before taking a left turn. This presents me with my first serious decision as I am by now decidedly disinclined to explore the region unnecessarily. I choose finally to believe the sign rather than the map, but it isn't until I actually arrive at the hostel that my decision is revealed to have been the right one.

At 62, this is my first experience of youth hostelling and I rather tentatively register myself in with the very jolly warden, Kathy, who seems to be not only the warden, but also the cook, receptionist and mother to all and sundry. She is warm and welcoming and tells me which room I am in.

Until I walked into the youth hostel in St Just I have to admit that I have given hardly any thought at all, even when planning my trip, to hostel conditions. The extent of my knowledge is that they are cheaper than anywhere else to stay, if you don't count a tent.

Whatever I imagined it is not what greets me as I push the door open. Later, when I have acclimatised to my new surroundings I realise that I must have been expecting an empty room with one bed, because I'm completely put out by the sight that awaits me. In the smallish room there are six bunks, five of them with outdoor gear strewn on them, rucksacks and great big boots on the floor, hefty anoraks hanging from anything projecting upwards, towels draped everywhere and not a hanger or hook to be seen. The remaining unoccupied bunk is mine, up the ladder, with not a single inch of anywhere to put anything. I am aghast! It all looks so masculine! Am I sleeping with five men? Or have I mistaken the room? I hurry downstairs and rather embarrassedly enquire whether it is hostel policy to mix the sexes? Not that that would be a problem, I hasten to add, not wishing to seem too uncool for words, but I would just like to know. Oh no, says Kathy, they're all girls!

I feel a complete lemon… it's only when I get back to the room that I notice the sign on the door which might have saved me from embarrassment.

My confusion dealt with, my thoughts turn to food. Although I can book breakfast for the following day, I am too late for a hostel-cooked meal tonight. So supper is a tin of macaroni cheese I buy on the premises and heat up in the self-catering kitchen. Food plays a large part in my life at home, cooking and eating a pleasure to share with family and friends, but on this journey it will prove to have a more basic function. Doing this trip is about paring things back, about just being and so food becomes fuel rather than fun.

In the hostel kitchen, a couple of young Germans are cooking blackberries that they have picked earlier. Although I think it odd to cook them, rather than eat them raw, the smell is wonderful and I resolve to do the same another day. It has been the best year ever for blackberries apparently and I love the idea of foraging for nature's gifts. Eating supper in the peaceful garden, overlooking the hills in the distance, is unforgettable. Calm has descended on the day and at last on me.

Later, when the sun has set on my first day on the road, I chat to a young German girl in the 'dorm'. All my room-mates are young and German but Carola is the only one of them who speaks English and, like me, she is travelling on her own. But though she is also on two wheels hers are attached to a great big motorbike. She tells me that she likes England a lot, and is living in Sandhurst. She has a job in a call centre and, afterwards, my curiosity belatedly aroused, I wish I had asked her more about it. Call centres seem to employ a lot of people, and I just can't imagine how they work. Do they sit in rows with earphones on, as typists used to do in 'pools'? How many people are there answering the phones? Dozens or hundreds? I am surprised when she tells me that it is easier to find work over here than in Germany at the moment. I have since learned that London is a magnet for young people, and as the grand-daughter of an immigrant Armenian who came to England at the end of the 19th century, I am entirely in sympathy with people seeking work in what is still a land of opportunity.

Carola's four-day holiday is going to take her all over Cornwall and Devon. She complains it's so tiring! Oh really, I reply, rather drily!

After filling in my diary - a one-liner recording the 19 miles cycled today, part of the longer journey that's taken me from home in Harefield to St Just, with Land's End and the start of my journey in sight - I retire to bed at a modest 9.30, utterly but rather contentedly exhausted.

CHAPTER 3 - Land's End Ahoy!

The following morning, a full 24 hours after leaving home, I still haven't reached the start of my journey, and I can't wait to get going. After a full traditional breakfast I say good-bye to Carola and wish her luck with her future.

It is a perfect day for the adventure to begin - what I don't know at the time is that it will be one of the best of the trip - not only is there a warm hazy sunshine and an autumnal stillness in the air, but the nearer I get to my destination, the flatter the roads become and the clearer and more magical the light grows. The stretch of A30 I ride along is calmer than expected, very few cars and just one motorbike...

Carola draws up alongside me in all her black leather paraphernalia, looking extremely professional. I am most impressed. We exchange more greetings and adieus and then she's off in a cloud of noise, smoke and speed. I think of Aesop's Tortoise and Hare story and wonder which of us will actually reach Land's End first. Unsurprisingly, as I'm not a tortoise, it is her.

The atmosphere at Land's End on this particular day is so luminous that even the tourist presence in the form of the usual shops can't spoil it. There are only a few others here and they all, like me, seem to be spellbound by the quality of the light and the calm and quiet of the beautiful late summer weather. It is utterly magical.

I ask a young woman to take the mandatory photograph of me and the bike in front of the signpost saying 'John O'Groats 1078 miles' and pointing in the right direction.

I feel torn about leaving as I could easily spend the entire day here, but the arrival of the ubiquitous tourist coaches weaving their way into the car park provides the spur to an immediate departure. However, I'm so busy congratulating myself on my timing that I miss the B road I had planned to take back to Penzance, which follows closer to the sea than the busier A30 that I now have to take. Happily, though, it's not too busy.

I had also planned to take it really easy on my first day, and only to go as far as the Penzance youth hostel. However, the A30 is not just busier, it's also faster and I arrive in no time at all. But I can't find the hostel, so it means just cycling on, past the town on a designated cycle path adjacent to the beach for about two miles. It's a lovely ride, but just as I decide to stop for a swim and a leisurely picnic lunch on the beach, the sun goes behind the clouds and it suddenly feels too chilly - the best of the day is over already.

Swimming and picnic cancelled, I take a short break to eat a snack in a car park instead and then it's on to Marazion, a very pretty little town overlooking St. Michael's Mount, which begs to have its photo taken, so I oblige.

Once through Marazion I turn away from the sea and join the B3280. This is one of the routes recommended by the Cyclists' Touring Club, and striking away from the main roads into the unknown hinterland, I need the reassurance of their recommendation. For goodness sake! I am now cycling much further than I planned for my second day and my next task is to find somewhere to stay. It's only mid afternoon, but tiredness is creeping up. Although I spotted numerous B&B signs around Marazion, it is evident I have now passed out of the holidaymaking area into farmland. Relubbus and Townshend offer nothing, and I'm becoming slightly anxious after a 27-mile ride with just one 10-minute break, when I thankfully see a large welcoming B&B sign in Leedstown.

As I mark it on my map, the distance between Land's End and Leedstown looks a long way, and I feel inordinately pleased with myself. But I also feel so tired, and spend half an hour just resting on the bed, staring mindlessly at the ceiling while my body adjusts to not sitting on a saddle. A very welcome cup of tea with fresh milk provided by my ever-so-kind landlady, Susan, combines with a hot bath to leave me feeling refreshed and normal once again.

Outside in the garden there's an inviting spot in the sun and I retire there to study the map for the next day and write up incredibly little about the day's progress.

When I go back inside I find a South African gentleman sitting in the lounge trying to find something on the television. His son back in South Africa has apparently just phoned him to say that they're thrashing England in the final test match. But he's having trouble finding any coverage on the TV. He gives up and talks to me instead, mainly about food, one of my favourite subjects.

After cycling all day, I have little inclination to travel far in search of supper, but I fancy something a little more substantial than last night's macaroni cheese. Susan has mentioned a nearby pub, that has recently been taken over by new management and of which she has heard good reports. Not wanting to move more than 100 yards from my bed puts me at the mercy of whatever happens to be nearby. And at

the mercy of the 'new management' is certainly how I feel. Tinned potatoes (instantly identifiable as such though I have never, to my knowledge, eaten a tinned potato) with no vestige of flavour or seasoning, a slab of spicy chicken, dry and very un-chicken-shaped, looking instead as if it had been cut from a loaf, and a 1950s salad consisting of a damp lettuce leaf, a thick slice of cucumber and half a tomato. Dressings, unappetising and vinegary, come in plastic pouches. It is dire and depressing. I wonder if it is me, just being fussy, but when I discuss my meal with my new South African acquaintance, I discover that his experience mirrored mine and he is in total agreement.

While food is not a major item on my agenda on this trip, I do find myself indignant with this country where we still serve up, and charge people for, badly cooked food. I can't believe it still happens. Such ignorance and indifference surely makes us the worst country in the world for food. Historically, this doesn't seem to have been the case. Somewhere or other it has gone wrong.

Fortunately our faith is restored the following morning when Susan provides the most generous of traditional breakfasts. She also provides me with painkillers for a neck ache which has bothered me since the previous afternoon. Her generosity extends, too, to offering help at any time on my journey should I need it. I know she means it when she tells me to give them a ring if I get into trouble.

My trip has also been of interest to the South African's companion who comes from Zimbabwe. She says that she's envious of me, but wonders why I'm on my own. I tell her that if I'd tried hard enough I could have found a companion, but that I rather relished the challenge of being entirely responsible for myself.

It is in fact much more than just the challenge, but it's not until I've completed the journey that I see clearly why I needed to do it and just what made me take to the road. She meanwhile understands completely, but says she thinks I am brave.

I think *she's* brave, to be living in Zimbabwe. I tell her I'd be frightened to death in that situation. Then she says something surprising. She says that although she feels frightened she also feels privileged to be living there through these times. It strikes me as an extremely positive approach, though I think privileged is a strange, unexpected word to use and wish afterwards that I could have spoken to her at length about it.

The four of us say good-bye as if we had known each other for much longer than a few hours. Yet we hadn't even exchanged names! It's one of the oddities of travelling that you don't need to know someone's name to have a deep and interesting conversation, or to remember them long afterwards.

As a parting shot, the gentleman tells me that apparently his son had just been winding him up about the cricket. It hasn't even started yet!

CHAPTER 4 - He Who Pays The Ferryman …

It's another gloriously sunny morning. How much longer can this wonderful weather last? The longer it continues the more important it becomes to get a few days' enjoyable pedalling behind me, without it having to be too character building! To feel that I have achieved *something* at least. No main roads today, just little lanes, as I'm trying to travel south Cornwall rather than north. So I'm aiming for Falmouth and crossing the bay to St. Mawes by ferry, which I just fancy doing on such a beautiful day. And, until the reality of my whim becomes clear, the alternative route has a greater difficulty factor, at least in terms of the cycling.

I need my intuition to guide me through the lanes though, as my map is inadequate and I'm sure I'm going round in circles some of the time. My years as a gardener and a modicum of common sense tell me that I have to make sure the sun is either to my right or behind me. What navigation! Some of these lanes are very narrow, and the hedges too high to see over. I feel vulnerable to local traffic which always travels too fast and too confidently, and I make myself get a move on, but fortunately there isn't as much as I fear. I get used to asking directions from anybody who's available, and also enjoy two or three miles actually riding without walking. Up to now, it seems as if about 50 per cent of my progress has been on my feet rather than on my derrière.

One of the principal reasons for conducting my odyssey on the saddle of a bicycle – apart of course from pedalling in Dervla Murphy's shadow - is that an arthritic foot makes walking less than comfortable – my days in Cornwall saw me battling up hills using the bike as a makeshift zimmer frame and I was always thrilled to have my feet firmly on the pedals instead of on the ground.

The A road from Penryn to Falmouth is quite dreadful from a cyclist's point of view, but Falmouth, once reached, is a sweet town and once again a glorious light is reflected off the sea - the gulls, boats and fishermen all combining to create a wonderful harbour atmosphere. I eat my lunch on a bench watching it all in the warm sunshine and waiting for the ferry. When the time comes I join the queue, shuffling forwards towards the boat.

Then suddenly, to my consternation, I notice what I have failed to consider as I lazed in the sunshine - the steps leading down to the boat are extremely steep and narrow (just like the lanes - typically Cornish!) and at the bottom they turn at a sharp right angle to get on to the boat.

My groundless fears at Slough Station fade into nothingness compared with what I'm now facing. As my panniers weigh an absolute ton I sense a potential disaster and I ask three strong looking young men if they can help.

'Sure, no problem', they say. It's almost the *last* thing they say. Even though their spirit is willing and their combined flesh far from weak, the next few moments are sheer hell. The bike almost runs amok even with the four of us struggling to keep it under control. If we lose it about six people ahead of us will be pushed down the steps, probably to their final destination.

Somehow or other, sheer fear gives us the strength to get the bike on board but my heart is already pounding at the thought of getting it off! Having faced the very real possibility of becoming a modern day Charon, ferryman to the dead en route to Hades, the ferryman is none too pleased and says I must remove the panniers before he will allow the bike to be carried off. I adamantly refuse to take the panniers off, and then have the rather belated brainwave of removing their insides, as I do in the evenings.

I must have felt so relaxed sitting in the sun and watching the world go by, that my brain just fell asleep. I am not a happy bunny during the crossing, the bike is getting in everyone's way and even though I've removed the panniers' contents, I'm still apprehensive about getting everything off, safely and without making a complete fool of myself. But as it turns out, people are helpful and there is no great drama. The ferryman himself has mellowed on the crossing and actually does most of the lifting, while other folk bring the bags up and nobody is killed!

CHAPTER 5 - No Room At The Inn

St Mawes is on the Roseland peninsula and at the very end of the Roseland Heritage Coast. In my flusterment on arrival there, and my relief at having survived the ferry crossing against considerable odds, I manage to drag the bike two sides of a triangle up the hill towards Trewithian without first checking the layout of the town.

I meet the three young men who came to my rescue on the ferry coming in the other direction, and thank them as I have completely forgotten to do before. They seem to bear no rancour towards me for the struggle I caused them. Like so many Cornish villages, St Mawes is appealingly attractive, but I don't give myself a chance to explore it fully, traipsing instead up yet another hill out of the town. As soon as possible and with a huge sense of relief, I leave the main road and plunge into the little lanes, cycling for about five miles in absolute peace and quiet.

From the very beginning I have decided to stop each day before I feel I have to, reckoning that three o'clock would be a good time to start looking for accommodation. But today, three o'clock comes and goes. It's so easy just to keep going in a rather mindless way, which would be fine if I knew exactly where tonight's bed was.

Part of the trouble, I realise later, is that I haven't been eating properly. Drinking lots of water, yes, and usually managing the protein with big breakfasts, and fresh fruit bought on the hoof so to speak. But I should be eating more carbohydrates during and after the ride and I haven't taken that into account in my planning.

At about four I come to Veryan, on the outskirts of which I meet a lady tending her garden. Asking her if there is a B&B in the village she shakes her head and says she doesn't know. There's something about her that gives me the impression she's a weekender. I think I must be right when, ten seconds later, just round the corner, there is the sign!

As a gardener myself I understand her preoccupation entirely, and sympathise with how easy it is sometimes to miss the bigger picture when concentrating on the search for omens of life or death in the plant kingdom.

Pleasure quickly turns to disappointment. The B&B is so sorry but they are full - so they say. Probably they would prefer to have a double booking. A nearby guest house is also sorry. And so is the landlord of the local inn. Everyone is sorry - but none of them as sorry as me. The next village shown on the map is about seven miles away, far too far in my present state, so I have to ponder my next move. First priority - a quiet nervous breakdown. I'm feeling quite miserable as my neck still aches, in large part I'm sure because I have a rucksack (albeit a very light one) on my back. Then a voice calls out behind me from the direction of the pub. They have a single, if that is any good! The landlord had assumed it was a double that was wanted, but his wife has told him to find out exactly what I'm looking for. With some difficulty I manage to maintain my dignity and refrain from kissing his feet.

A hot bath and a cup of tea later, I feel refreshed enough to plan tomorrow's route (if plan is the right word). Today's 24 miles are again satisfactory and I treat myself to an appetizing pub meal rather than snacking in my room with only the television for company. I spend the rest of the evening strolling around the village in the sunshine, although I manage to miss Veryan's star attractions, the five round thatched cob (mud) houses built in the 1820s by the Reverend Jeremiah Trist for his daughters. I learn later that there are two at each end of the village and one in the middle, all of them still lived in. Each has a cross on the roof and legend has it that they were built round so there were no corners for the devil to lurk in.

Even before setting off next morning, cycling is the main theme of conversation at breakfast. With me in their midst, talk among us all turns to cycling and one of the other guests comments that cyclists can't complain, not that I do so, about a lack of cycle paths, since they don't pay any road tax. I think about this - apart from the fact that cycles don't pollute the environment with toxic emissions or noise, and the wear and tear on road surfaces is minimal - and come to the conclusion that he doesn't have a leg to stand on.

I have always imagined that the road tax paid by motorists fails to meet the cost of maintaining existing roads or of building new ones, so that a good proportion of the money needed comes from general taxation. But it seems I am wrong and that the money raised from the motorists far exceeds that used on roads. Winston Churchill was apparently the first Prime Minister to syphon off road tax for other purposes, and it still happens. If this is so, then in my view motorists should complain about this, rather than getting irritated by cyclists, who are as often as not also car owners and as such pay road tax anyway.

It is an educational breakfast and I learn something else that I tuck away. When the conversation turns to a discussion about arthritis I am advised that a knob of stem ginger every day can help. I decide to give it a try when I get home.

With or without ginger, my neck still aches and I make a mental note for next time - do not cycle with a rucksack, however light.

CHAPTER 6 - The Garden Of Eden

My overall planning is favouring southern routes over northern ones in the hope that I can meet up with some of my family holidaying near Babbacombe Bay next week. Which means that I am heading in the general direction of Dartmoor, a prospect which looms rather ominously in my mind, Slough Station syndrome once again. Pushing the thought aside, I resolve to take each day as it comes, and concentrate my efforts for the day on getting to the Golant youth hostel on the other side of St Austell.

I enjoy an uneventful ride to St Austell, where the helpful staff at the Tourist Office give me complicated directions to Golant the pretty way via Par, rather than through the town and along the main roads. Indeed, it is a very pretty route, passing through Charleston, a town with a Shipwreck & Heritage Centre, old classic ships in its harbour and a fish smokery. The smoked pepper mackerel bought for my supper will turn out to be the best, most succulent and tasty I have ever eaten. Before then I meander around the town eating my first Cornish ice cream.

Then it's back in the saddle and up more hills and down again to Gerrans Bay, its beach supposedly part of a designated cycle route! While I am standing in the middle of the sand dunes wondering where on earth I am supposed to go, some kindly folk point me towards a small car park. The lane snakes up and away round a corner so steeply it almost curves round and back over my head, like a surfer's Big One. Obviously it's a cycle route because it's simply too steep for cars!

The next three miles to Golant are best glossed over, lost and forgotten in the detritus of my memory. It's enough to say Tywardreath is rather hilly. It calls above all for perseverance – so I grit my teeth, keep going and eventually reach my destination. The hostel, in common with so many others, is in a quiet rural setting down a mile-long track. This one has educational facilities and there are lots of colourful letters displayed on the wall from school children to the warden, thanking him for all sorts of exciting and intriguing activities. Like night games.

I am fast becoming an expert on youth hostelling so I now know that hostels are not manned until five in the evening; if you arrive before that time without having booked, you can pop your membership card into an envelope provided (the number of envelopes left indicates the number of available beds left that night) and put it on the desk. This guarantees you a bed and you can go away if you wish and return anytime before 10 pm when the doors shut. I pop my membership card into an available envelope and leave it on the desk, thus ensuring my reservation.

Sitting quietly in the sun out in the garden slowly but surely restores my equilibrium. Only 23 miles 'cycled' today, but although it was a fairly short ride, it was an exhausting one. My plan for tomorrow is to spend the entire day at the Eden Project, just six miles from Golant, and stay a second night at this same hostel. The question is should I cycle there and enjoy a £3.50 reduction on the entrance ticket, or should I walk the mile up the track, another mile along a lane to the cross roads to catch the bus to St Austell, then another bus to Eden? Doing the environmental thing by cycling is tempting, but the weather forecast that evening makes my mind up for me. It is not good. And Sunday, the day after that, is even worse. Rain is forecast for the Saturday, gales and storms for Sunday. Spending a day on the buses and inside the biomes at the Project seems infinitely more compelling than cycling in the rain. Besides which, I want to enjoy what is there in a fresh state of mind and body.

I spend the evening in front of a big fire that has been lit in the lounge, enjoying a relaxed and pleasant conversation with Catherine, who is holidaying with her two grown-up children, enjoying the last of the summer before they return to their respective universities.

In spite of the forecast, Saturday dawns bright and fresh again, though it still fails to tempt me into the saddle. Instead I reach Eden via two bus rides, the second being the special from St Austell. All the towns roundabout have dedicated buses to Eden, all of them selling entrance tickets, and the bus journey provides the first indication of a most impressive organisation that has perfected the art of dealing with thousands of visitors quickly and smoothly. Sitting smugly on the nearly empty bus, I am thankful not to be on my bike - the roads are, as ever, very beautiful, but as hilly as they are beautiful and six miles each way would have been a mistake for a day which is supposed to be a break!

Right from the very beginning, from the bus stop, past the car parks and into the ticket/reception areas, there is ample evidence of well-thought-out and imaginative design. Planting, sculpture, sign-posting are clear, pleasing, fun and informative. The cafés inside carry the same message - environmental responsibility can be beautiful as well as practical. Tables, chairs, cardboard mugs, graphics, posters, and the lavatories - all the little details which usually let a project down - are considered, not just for utility but also for their aesthetics. It also looks clean and well-maintained. It has the effect, even if it's unconscious, of making a person at ease with their surroundings, even if it only banishes the usual irritations of sloppy maintenance.

Everything is about plants and our relationship to them and I spend the day absorbing a wealth of fascinating facts and figures. It is very educational, in a fun kind of way, not a bit like the geography lessons of my childhood. I learn that the planet grows more sugar cane than wheat, that carob seeds were carat weight for gold and that nicotine is the most widely used of all drugs with more than 15 billion cigarettes smoked every day worldwide by more than a third of adults.

In the Mediterranean biome a tall, slim black actor, dressed in a long flowing white robe tells the story of how the world began - I've forgotten most of it but seem to remember it's something to do with monkeys and fingers. Anyway, it looks and sounds very dramatic and his spontaneous audience appreciates the unexpected theatre.

Equally fascinating as I wander around are the people. It is very hot under the biomes and everyone I see seems to be positively wilting in the heat, burdened by their bodies, bent and drooping. How lovely it would be for a moment to be nothing but spirit, I think.

As I wait for the little diddy train to take us back up to the exit, I enjoy a delicious, real, Cornish pasty, and food continues to exert temptation as I pick lots of juicy blackberries walking back down the lane to the hostel. Now that I have been introduced to the delights of cooked blackberries, it seems to be the only thing to do with them for tomorrow's breakfast.

Once again I spend the evening with Catherine and her son and daughter, Nick and Clare. I learn that they are from Edgbaston which, coincidentally, is where Will comes from originally. The four of us play cards for most of the evening – they teach me to play cheat while I reciprocate with lessons in how to play rummy. They are very good company, great fun to be with – and very sharp. I have to keep my addled wits about me to keep up with them!

If the gales arrive tomorrow, I resolve to have another day off and make myself cosy in the hostel with books.

CHAPTER 7 - Dampened Spirits

The predicted gales have not materialised, just gentle drizzle, so there's no excuse but to tog up and set off, all tempting thoughts of a cosy day reading by the fire abandoned. It doesn't take long to become soaked through, and by the time Lostwithiel becomes greyly visible through the mist at about 10 am, I am ready to call it a day. I cycle slowly round the little town hoping to catch some sign of life, but it's a Sunday and it's utterly miserable, and so totally different from yesterday. What to do? Even if I were to find a B&B I simply cannot give in so early - it would be so limp! Hang around until the coffee shop opens at 11? Too boring and cold. As I shelter shivering under a (closed) shop's awning a Tourist Information sign wavers into view - at least they might be open.

It's more than open - it's bursting at the seams with activity. People are bustling about preparing for a car boot sale - inside. There's a hatch where hot drinks and snacks are being served and an atmosphere of steamy bonhomie prevails. This is the place to be for the next hour or so, in the hope the rain might ease off. As usual, I fall into conversation with other people, and express my anxiety about the next 12 miles to Liskeard. I hardly dare ask, is it very, very hilly? Are there plenty of places to shelter along the way in case the weather turns even worse? Everybody contributes suggestions and advice. After a while, having downed an enormous mug of tea, dried out sufficiently to cheer myself up, and the rain having eased off, I reluctantly leave the cosy and eccentric Tourist Information Office, and set off for Liskeard. The clouds are thick and grey, but keep their wet load to themselves for now.

I pass by Liskeard, and through a village called Merrymeet, such a Tolkein-esque name that I fancifully wonder if Hobbits live there - warm and snug as Hobbits know so well how to be - and arrive at St Ive having cycled just under 24 miles. This is enough for today as I'm having to adjust my distances to allow a full day's cycling from Tavistock, the last town before Dartmoor, which I want to get across in one day, the day after next. A B&B sign leads to a house where I'm shown the accommodation. In the damp state I'm in, I'm ready to say yes to anything. But it's treat time. Because part of the house is being 'improved', the only place for me is a self-contained flat with a well-equipped kitchen. And all for the price of a normal room. The lounge has windows on three sides with a wonderful view of hills and sky. This is a generous couple who are not hanging around waiting for a better deal to come along; they have just taken me in, and organised a place where the bike can be secured for the night.

The lounge is so big that there's plenty of room on the floor for spreading all the maps out and for endless speculation on possible routes. What I'm searching for is the perfect, flat, traffic-free, beautiful route by-passing all big towns all the way to John O'Groats! Crossing Dartmoor, rather than Exmoor or Bodmin Moor, is now a certainty, but nevertheless I feel none too happy about the prospect of bad weather and free range ponies. Not being a rural sort of person, I quail at meeting creatures who are as free to roam as I am. But - onwards and upwards. Especially upwards! This trip is not meant to be without challenges. And more than one hundred miles have already been traversed, roughly one tenth of the trip!

I wallow in the unexpected luxury of a television that can be watched from the living room *and* the kitchen while preparing supper with goodies from the well-stocked fridge. An old film is on with Keith Michell as Henry VIII, and Charlotte Rampling and Jane Asher as two of his wives. The two women on the screen look barely any younger than they do now, even though the film must have been made in the 60's. How do they do it? It must be their bone structure. After 116 miles on the road, I'm feeling my age!

The next morning finds me dithering as the drizzle comes and goes and I'm none too keen to go out in it. The sky is well and truly thick with fast moving cloud and the thought of staying in my cosy nest, watching TV and maybe chatting to my hosts for the morning is so tempting. The weather could go either way, but the forecast seems to bear little relation to what is happening in this particular spot. It's supposed to be clearing up with warm bright spells. Definite proof of this would be most welcome, but one has to try to be optimistic, so....

One last cup of coffee drunk, a picnic prepared, then it's off. My nice host adjusts my panniers for me – I guess that, being an ex-marine, he knows about these things - wishes me luck, then returns to his garden to commune with his last surviving cat. He, his wife and their cat, will be moving soon, as too many of their beloved moggies have been mown down by traffic roaring along the A390. It's heartbreaking.

I enjoy, if that's the word, an uneventful ride to Tavistock, stopping only for 10 minutes to eat a small picnic standing up gazing over what surely would be lovely countryside if it could be seen. Uneventful that is, apart from the small, but oh so significant crossing of the county boundary into Devon on a bridge over the River Tamar. It feels greatly encouraging to have cycled the length of Cornwall.

I'm soaked through again by the time I reach Tavistock in the early afternoon and, as it's too late to cross Dartmoor today, this is definitely the place to stop. The Tourist Information Office just manages to find me a room, albeit a twin. The town is full of visitors, and with only three singles in it the bullet has to be bitten and a twin paid for. It's annoying having to pay almost double, particularly when the room is so small that if there *were* two people in it there would be nowhere to put their suitcases. *And*, what's more, it feels vaguely dishonest to me when they carve out a corner from an already small room to put a tiny shower and loo in, so they can call it 'en suite' and charge even more for the privilege of sleeping with one's nose half way down an S bend!

If Will were with me now, he would find my reaction all too familiar. Whenever we go away on holiday, I spend the first couple of days picking holes in everything – from the standard of the cleaning to the colour of the curtains. On one never-to-be-forgotten occasion we'd travelled to a particularly beautiful Scottish island, only for me to immediately berate poor Will with my strident views on how completely spoiled it was by the sewage on the beach.

When I finally came to a halt he patiently pointed out my mistake: "It's not sewage," he said. "It's black sand."

Despite my sorry condition I'm offered nothing in the way of drying facilities, but I am allowed to borrow an umbrella and go to explore the town on foot. It looked very interesting on the way in but 'on foot' is not something my feet are up to today, so doing historic buildings and shopping slip quietly off the agenda. I opt instead for an early night, feeling seriously disgruntled at the state of the UK's tourist industry.

CHAPTER 8 - Famliar Faces

Breakfast the following morning is in the much advertised conservatory which looks lovely in the photo but is a bit on the chilly side on a damp sunless morning. But it has an attractive view down the garden to the river. Our hostess fusses over us solicitously, but somehow it all lacks warmth and atmosphere.

Feeling slightly apprehensive, I depart for the big push across Dartmoor, and almost immediately outside Tavistock the moor begins. The weather is overcast but at least it's dry, and the views are wonderful. It's a slog up a long, shallow climb, but the higher I go the further I can see and the more wondrous it becomes. The air smells fresh and clean, and in between the not-too-numerous cars it is quiet and peaceful. The turf that stretches away on either side looks so inviting for walkers, a few of whom I glimpse now and then getting out of cars and striding off with their dogs. I add this to the list of places I want to come back to as I would love to get to know the area better.

Sighting a mast it occurs to me that this could be a good place to try to ring my family who are somewhere in the vicinity of Babbacombe, and I get through on excellent reception. We arrange to meet at the youth hostel at Bellever (roughly 13 miles from Tavistock) in the early afternoon. I must be getting fitter as, in the event, I find I've modestly overestimated how long it will take me to get there and I reach the hostel about lunchtime. It's tucked away a mile off the road and I'm immediately convinced that my lovely family won't find it. My lovely family, on this occasion, comprises Ben, my son, his girlfriend Sarah, my daughter Beccy, her husband Neil and their daughter, our first grandchild, Evie, who is two and a bit. I deposit the bike in the security of the hostel's barn, and walk back up the track, munching an apple and cheese for lunch. I can't ring them here as there is no mobile signal so I just have to wait until they turn up. Which they do just as I'm beginning to turn blue with cold. It's lovely to see them, and they are agog to know how I am and what's been happening. We have a gorgeous walk around Postbridge which is almost empty. It's a beautiful spot with a Tolkien-esque bridge, rocks and tumbling water and lovely mossy banks to walk on which would be completely covered with people if it were a few degrees warmer. Then on to, of all places, a pub, for a Devonshire cream tea, then a pony centre which we discover has shut early for the day. We return in the direction of the hostel, stopping for a bracing walk across to one of the many tors.

Then I am taken back to the hostel for the night but, once there, I am persuaded that I should have a few creature comforts for tonight, and go back with them to their holiday home, where there is a convenient spare room.

Having checked that it's all right for me to leave the bike for the night at the hostel, we do just that. Opting for a night of comfort serves another, very useful purpose. It's a valuable research trip as we are travelling the road I shall have to do the next day to Moretonhampstead.

A delicious dinner appears by magic, the first real meal I have eaten for several days. It's nice to have some familiar company and after an evening of t.l.c. I feel like a new woman.

Lovely as the interlude is, however, it has left me feeling slightly unsettled. My journey has somehow been disrupted, in the nicest possible way, but disrupted nonetheless. It's as if, by letting them persuade me out of staying at the hostel, I have relinquished control of my journey and fallen back into letting other people make decisions for me, just when I was getting the hang of making them for myself.

I feel I have let myself down slightly by relinquishing full control – of slipping back into my comfort zone when getting out of it is what the trip is all about.

CHAPTER 9 - Alone Again

Ben and Sarah drive me back to Bellever to collect the bike. They wait until I have repacked the panniers and sorted myself out, which includes putting on everything I have, as the weather is quite cold and unpleasant. The last they see of me, as they slowly pass me in the car waving wildly and encouragingly, is plodding up the lane towards the main road, in the drizzle, head down and appearing, I should imagine, rather a solitary figure.

I'm sure they felt more iffy for me than I felt for myself. I could see they were a little unhappy leaving me on my own in the damp, grey drizzle, but I had a job to do and I wanted to get on and do it. I was actually feeling very rested and quite exhilarated at the thought of the coming ride over the rest of Dartmoor.

Although the road is easier than yesterday, the weather is not. Gusty wind and a misty outlook makes the views disappear, but at least it's mostly downhill. I reach Moretonhampstead far more quickly than anticipated, and have an early lunch of soup and rolls in a café. '

I wish I had time to explore the villages on the edge of Dartmoor - Chagford, Great Weeke, Throwleigh, and to visit Castle Drogo, but that would all take at least another day, and my plans don't allow for that. But the B3212 continues to Dunsford, and it's a beautiful ride through wooded lanes and manicured villages - there are so many places to "ooh and ah" over that I have to concentrate to stay focused on the goal! I'm making a mental note though, to return to Dartmoor to do more cycling another time, as it's been such a pleasure to experience it on the bike as opposed to seeing it flash by from a car window. The scenery is glorious, even if the weather is not, and it is not too crowded, nor so empty that I am frightened. On a nice day and with a following wind one should be able to cross it comfortably in a day.

I spend the night in a café/B&B, and there discover I have left my mobile transformer at the Tavistock B&B. I'm furious with myself, especially as I suspect it was my negative thinking about the cost of staying in Tavistock which made me take my eye off the ball for a moment. Interspersed with fury is panic but fortunately I can use the public phone on the landing, and I get through to my former landlady and arrange for it to be forwarded on to the youth hostel at Street.

However, when I phone Street to book a night on Saturday and to ask them to keep a packet which will, I hope optimistically, arrive in the post for me, I'm told they are fully booked on Saturday and Sunday and closed on Monday and Tuesday. This means I must reach Street by Friday evening, giving me just two days to cycle 76 miles. As I've never travelled more than 30 miles in a single day, and that was more than 20 years ago, I have a bit of a challenge on my hands. It's a good thing the terrain is gradually levelling out a bit.

'Dinner' is a snack sitting on the bed watching the box and resting up for two days' hard travelling.

Just a young man and me at breakfast, and it seems a bit too 'English' just to sit and eat in silence, so I instigate a conversation and ask him if he's on holiday.

No, he tells me, he's a representative for Yellow Pages and his job is to visit schools encouraging them to sign up to the Yellow Pages schools recycling scheme, which sounds like a good idea to me.

He chatters on endlessly about himself, but before saying goodbye he tells me how interesting it has been talking to me!

There's no way to avoid passing through Exeter, unless I by-pass it to Tiverton but...I know some of the lanes around and about that town, very 'Cornish', and besides it would be floating too far north for my plans. I know that tricky navigation will be needed to get through Exeter, but by following the CTC instructions I'm hoping all will go smoothly. I have become so used to being in the unpolluted fresh country air all day long, for over a week, that I'm not looking forward to a city environment at all. Any city. But particularly not Exeter. The road from Dunsford to the outskirts of Exeter was very nice indeed, but it proved to be a tasty hors d'oeuvre to an indigestible main course. Not only does Exeter not have a ring road, I discover it doesn't have any cycle lanes either. Following the CTC instructions to the letter, I plod through suburbs and negotiate roundabouts and endure speedy traffic to the left of me, to the right of me, and behind me until I am thankfully free of this wretched unfriendly-to-cyclists, noisy, unattractive city.

This is the fifth day of an overcast, oppressive sky and I need to see the sunshine again. Cornwall in the sun is so much nicer than Devon in the rain and I am looking back on my first few days with nostalgia.

It is sometime during this day that, having dismounted for a moment, and leant my bike against me to study the map, the front wheel does its own thing, spinning round and nearly toppling the bike completely on its side. Maps and papers fly out of the handlebar bag on to the road. Precariously balancing my laden bike - it's not a good idea to lay a laden bike down on its side - I bend down to pick everything up, but fail to notice that my second pair of reading glasses and sun specs have also dropped out. When I realise this in the evening, I begin to wonder if I should be let out on my own.

As my nights on the road mount up I realise that I am approaching each night's B&B with a critical and resentful attitude, ready to find fault. I have quickly learned to read the hidden meanings of signs offering 'en suite' accommodation – they'll be twice the price! Places with signs offering only the bed and breakfast prove, in my experience, to be slightly more down-at-heel, but infinitely more welcoming, obviously valuing warmth, friendliness and an interest in people above the financial rewards of a shower cubicle shoe-horned into a cupboard.

I hope I manage to conceal my misgivings from my hosts, as I invariably feel sad by the following morning to be leaving a warm and familiar nest! How perverse is the human heart.

Following the CTC instructions once more I wend my way along quiet lanes through Dog Village, Whimple and Tallaton to Fenny Bridges, and finally to a farmhouse from Victorian times. This is where all the missing sparrows are, along with ducks, geese, ponies and children's play area, wild garden, shop and tea house … and a warm welcome and a safe place for a bike.

It's a rickety old house, full of dilapidated, lived-in charm, and books. I have a large room with TV. After a long hot bath I'm ready for nothing more exciting than my usual evening routine of munching on snacks and channel-hopping. Mindless but eminently enjoyable and as much as I can cope with for the day, having cycled nearly 28 miles. This is the most so far, almost equalling my long-ago record, but if I'm to get to Street tomorrow I shall have to cycle nearly 49 miles!

The good thing is that, as I have already booked my bed for tomorrow night, I can cycle long after I would normally stop, when the exhaustion that comes from the fear of not finding a bed for the night usually puts the brakes on for me.

CHAPTER 10 - The Longest Day

Breakfast is taken with an American couple who are big - he in height, she in girth. Fascinatingly, the general topic of conversation is the massive portions of food served in the US. They are eating a huge cooked breakfast and it is this that prompts their comments. I've been offered the same, but some misguided impulse to self-denial made me refuse in favour of some slow energy release porridge. I try hard to restrain my comments, aware that I myself am hardly the size I would like to be.

The farmer's wife and I have a 'grumpy old women' conversation, too, about one of my pet hates, in the course of which she reveals that she and her husband, like me, are not only computer illiterate but computer phobic too, and hate the microchip, Microsoft, plasma plastic global www.dot.com nature of today's so-called communication with a passion to rival mine. The idioglossia of text message language, and the domination of an unforgiving and authoritarian flickering screen which regularly informs the innocent writer that they have 'performed an illegal act' are, we agree, an affront to the human spirit! We have a soul-mate discussion of modern obscenities. This revelation of their values certainly explains the 'stepping back in time' ambience of their yard, the emphasis on life in the form of animals and birds, and the simple pleasure of growing simple things.

On being asked where I'm heading for that day I say I must get to Street that evening as I need to pick up my mobile phone transformer, which I'm hoping is waiting for me. Do you mean one of these things? she asks, bringing out from a drawer, indeed, one of those things. We have lots left here, I am told, would you like it? We check it is the right sort for my phone, find that it is and I accept the orphan. I feel complete again – what irony - with my very own modern obscenity!

Now for the big push. The next town is Honiton, reached on the old A30, a very pleasant but all-too-short ride. Rather than travel on the by-pass I go right through the centre, a long straight road with temptingly interesting upmarket shops. But there's no time for such frivolity, and it's too early to enjoy a cup of something in one of its numerous cafés. A pity, because when it *is* time there won't be one. Sod's law.

Although I do not by-pass Honiton, I do by-pass a friend who lives there. I would have liked to have had a cup of tea with her, but today of all days even a mile out of my way would be too much. And I have learned from meeting up with the family that socialising is too distracting, and makes my journey less my own.

After Honiton it is hell. There is no alternative but the A30 for a few miles and it really is a case of keeping as close to the hedgerow as possible, and sometimes even stopping to let a crawling lorry pass. The road is a single track each way with a continuous double white line down the middle. To call this an A road is ludicrous. Not only should it be a complete no-no for cyclists, it should be widened for motorists. Not that I have much sympathy for them at the moment, but I know that a quiet period of traffic will be followed by a lumbering lorry followed by a line of impatient cars and vans. Then there will be another blessed quiet period for a minute or two, until another monster crawls past.....But traffic does not like to cross the continuous line I notice, not even when there's nothing coming the other way. It would much rather brush me into the undergrowth! This stretch is ghastly and best forgotten.

Mercifully, a mile after Monkton the instructions take the cyclist into the lanes again. The sky is a beautiful blue, and it is so quiet that the sound of buzzing insects and the birds singing in the hedgerows suddenly becomes noticeably audible. The calmness of the day works its spell, and I realise that this is one of those memorable moments which I recognise at the time *is* a memorable moment! Instead of continuing to push the bike in a rushed and hurried way, I now slow down and savour the tranquillity. Gazing over the landscape and lazily munching an apple I think of 'this precious pearl set in a silver sea' and wish I could remember more than a few snatches of prose and poetry at a time. A happy moment and worth every laboured step.

Back on to a main road - the A303 - and it's another nightmare for about six miles. I'm too preoccupied with staying alive to notice or care that I've passed into Somerset somewhere along this stretch. All the same - that's two counties down! Then dalliances with more lanes and villages and complete disorientation for a while. My map is just not detailed enough, and the instructions confusing. A sign to Barrington Court appears and I wish I had time to visit it. After wandering around in a bit of a daze for about half an hour, I eventually manage to come across someone who actually gives me correct information.

The rest of the afternoon is spent enjoying a pleasant and uneventful journey to Street, relatively easy with wide lanes and little traffic. The map is clear, with little possibility of wrong turnings, and at the end of the day's ride only the long hill to Street to struggle up. The hostel nestles in woodland off the main road, just to the south of Glastonbury, it is 6 pm, the reception is open, and my packet has arrived!

Gratitude flows to my Tavistock landlady. I joke to the warden that I now have two transformers but no sun specs. That's no problem, he says, we've had a pair in our lost property for several weeks and it's very unlikely they'll be reclaimed now. He fishes in a drawer, then hands over a very trendy pair which fit perfectly. It seems only fair that I should contribute the extra transformer I acquired from the farm to the hostel.

This sharing of resources is something that characterises the life I am living – when I stay in youth hostels I often find a free breakfast, courtesy of people who have travelled through before me.

After nearly 49 miles of cycling today I am very relieved to have reached Street. The hostel is not full so I have the girls' room to myself. What bliss. After a hot shower comes the reorganisation of my bits and pieces and a long phone call to Will. Earlier I bumped into a tall young blond man called Paul coming in with his panniers, looking as I had felt an hour earlier. It hadn't taken long to discover that we are doing the same End-to-End ride, and we agree to swap notes later.

Paul and Geoff, a man Paul had met the previous evening in another hostel, and I have supper together, discussing the different routes (and times – he started on the Sunday after my Tuesday!) Paul and I have taken to arrive at the same place from the same starting point, and where we are heading the following day. Paul rode over Bodmin Moor instead of Dartmoor, and he waxed lyrical over its beauty.

Paul has raised nearly £1000 in sponsorship for various charities. For the first time, I wonder why I have never considered doing my ride for charity, but I realise that it would have given me simply too much to think about. I wonder, too, about why every walk, ride, bungee jump and haircut is sponsored nowadays, and refuse to feel guilty for riding not just unhelmeted, but unsponsored too. I come to the conclusion that there is still room to do things for oneself, room to make one's own private journey. And this is mine.

Paul has done very well, having left Land's End six days after I did, but so he should, being half my age. He books himself in to Slimbridge hostel for the following night while I plan to go across the Severn Bridge and up the Wye Valley via the Cheddar Gorge. I would feel happier, though, if I could book myself in somewhere in advance as tomorrow is Sunday. I don't fancy getting involved with the Bristol suburbs, unavoidable if I go through the Gorge, without a definite destination for the night. There are no youth hostels open at this time of year in this area, and when I ring the B&Bs on my list I find they are either shut or full (weekend, of course). Cheddar is a popular destination. I retire to bed in my usual state of not knowing precisely where I'm going the following day!

CHAPTER 11 - Temporarily In Tandem

I am still dithering when I meet up again with Geoff and Paul at breakfast. Paul suggests I try and make for Slimbridge as well, but I'm reluctant to saddle him with a trailer, which I'm bound to be. He copies out a route plan he's following and gives it to me, but I'm still glued to the idea of the Cheddar Gorge. It's been on my list of 'must sees' since the start, but if I can't book in anywhere along that route... I prepare the bike for departure, and on my way out say goodbye to them both.

Geoff is off back home, and they ask me what I've decided to do. I say rather weakly that I still haven't made up my mind. Seeing the looks on their faces, I decide then and there to try for Slimbridge. This means missing the Gorge and the Wye Valley altogether and I shall have to re-plot my intended route for the coming days. It will be another big hike but why not try? Having at last reached a decision, I rush inside excitedly to ask the warden to call and book me in, if possible, to the Slimbridge youth hostel. This is a service the hostels provide for members, which is fantastic. They will even book a string of hostels for you if you give them your route and dates.

Slimbridge does have room so, waving goodbye to the other two, I leave, feeling really fired up and enthused now that I know where I'm heading. Procrastination drains energy, and I feel so much better, even though I know I've set my sights too high. I don't dare to tot up the mileage to be covered, so I pass Glastonbury reluctantly, continuing firmly on to Wells where I have to stop to buy another map. Little do I know what's in store. The A39 out of Wells is the longest, most time-consuming and most exhausting hill I have yet come across. It is interminable, and I'm unutterably fed up by the time I eventually reach the top and start my glide down to the bottom. Halfway down I see two male cyclists straining their way up - with a long, long trail of traffic behind them. We acknowledge each other ruefully, but I'm full of admiration that they have the nerve to hold it all up.

Somewhere during the next few miles I spot a figure in front of me, and it's Paul. I put on a spurt, not wanting him to disappear forever in the distance without a greeting, and pass him at such speed I can't bear to waste the energy by slowing down. We travel a little way with me in front until I hear him call my name. I have gone past the left turn. I rejoin him to compare notes. He stopped at Glastonbury but must have passed me as I shopped in Wells. We agree to travel together with him leading the way, on condition that he doesn't worry if I lag behind. I have seen that he is not one of these cyclists who put their head down to the tarmac to break records, but cycles instead at a dignified and steady pace, and I really do not want to be a liability with my fidgety stop-start habits. But I can see that my missing the turn-off has worried him slightly. He is a caring soul. However, on we go for a few miles, in companionable single file, arriving at Keynsham, where - somewhere – there is a dedicated cycle route weaving its way between Bath and Bristol.

Paul assertively turns left for half a mile, then right along the high street, with me following in the belief that he knows where he's going. He doesn't! It seems neither of us is completely confident of our whereabouts at this precise moment, and nobody we ask seems to know either. I have become quite shocked at how ignorant local people often are about their own neighbourhoods. We decide to go on for another mile or so, up hill, down hill, and there before us is a huge roundabout and the Bristol by-pass. Paul suddenly realises he knows exactly where we are, but I am completely unwilling to travel along the by-pass roaring ceaselessly with traffic. I can't face it, and anyway I am sure that we took the wrong route when we turned left at the beginning of the town. We decide to go our separate ways, but discover that we can't swap mobile phone numbers, as neither of us can remember them! so we say goodbye and I promise to let Paul know from wherever I finish up at the end of the day that I'm all right.

So, loath though I am to re-trace my wheels, it seems the only way for me. Down hill, up hill, along the high street and left for half a mile (half a mile sounds so little in a car!), then I am back at the point where I believe we went wrong. But...now I'm not so sure at all. The alternatives don't look so convincing. But lo - there is a cycle shop! Absolutely and exactly what I need, when I need it. How rare. However, they do not tell me what I want to hear. They can't put me on to the cycle route as it is far too complicated, and not particularly close by. What I have to do is, surprise, surprise, cycle back up through the town, up hill, down hill, then down to the big roundabout again, then along the by-pass. WHAT! No, no, no, but yes, yes, yes, that is what has to be done. Paul - you were right after all!

They do however offer one bit of information, which helps more than words can say. "Before you get to the roundabout," they tell me. "You will see a bollard! Next to the bollard is a cycle route sign, looking as though it's pointing in exactly the opposite direction to the one you want. It will take you to traffic lights which will get you across all the nasty big roads and deposit you on the cycle route running parallel to the by-pass for a few miles, over a bridge and back onto the right side for Goose Green." And it does. This is part of the path I have been reading about, and it's very satisfying to have been able to use at least part of it.

By the time I arrive at Goose Green, having met just two other cyclists using this wondrous and humane route through the madness of the Bristol suburbs, tiredness is kicking in and it's obvious I'm not going to make it to Slimbridge. In the end I am so tired I get lost, and realise that even if I go off-piste it doesn't matter much, as long as I find somewhere to rest. Eventually, on the outskirts of Yate, is just the right guesthouse which has a single room, of all unlikely things, and wonder of wonders, it's available. The B&B nestles behind a general stores, which provides me with an exciting supper of sandwiches. I remember to ring Slimbridge YH, where Paul has yet to arrive, and ask them to pass on to Paul the message that I'm OK and to cancel tonight's bed and to book one for tomorrow instead. Although today's scenery hasn't been as stunning as I've become accustomed to, the sunset is a gorgeous fanfare of reds, oranges and yellows, bringing a day of the most perfect weather to a close.

This has been the most difficult day's search for a B&B, and I could have avoided it. I have a dear cousin, Roger, who lives in Bath – though I didn't know it at the time, I passed within five minutes of his home that afternoon. I was so tired that my resolve to avoid turning my journey into a social trip would have been broken if I'd known, and I'd have rung him without a second thought!

CHAPTER 12 - Days Of Wine And Feathered Friends

Having failed to reach Slimbridge yesterday, I have not gone far enough to have lost the option to wend my way to the Severn Bridge and thence the Wye Valley, as originally planned. Because my detour has knocked Cheddar Gorge off my list, I decide to stick to the revised route and treat myself to Slimbridge.

It's a wonderful, wonderful day. Knowing exactly where I'm going does help and it's a relatively short and easy cycle ride in the perfect sunshine to get there. And then a trip to the nearby bird sanctuary to look forward to in the afternoon; it's a perfect marriage of anticipation and realisation.

Everything turns out as I hope. The Slimbridge hostel is empty, but open, and I relieve the bike of its luggage, wash some clothes and hang them up in the warm drying room (another useful facility offered by youth hostels), store my food in the fridge and make myself a cup of tea and lunch in the well-equipped kitchen. I take it outside and eat it in the shade of a tree, quietly enjoying the peace and watching the pond and bird life around me.

I have wanted to visit Sir Peter Scott's Wildfowl and Wetlands Trust for a long time, so I am very much looking forward to having such a perfect opportunity to go there. It's only a mile away, across the canal bridge and the marshes, a pleasant, level ride, which only takes a few minutes. There is a relatively new visitors' centre which has won various architectural awards, something that's of particular interest to me, since Will is an architect and it was in an architect's practice that we first met! From the outside the centre is a pale coloured timber and glass structure, and from the inside it is light and spacious and airy, the design reflecting the entirely appropriate feel of an aviary. It's a pleasure to be here.

I do notice however that, although a wooden-framed cupboard holding medals and such like has a brass plaque inscribed to its designer, there's no sign - anywhere - of the names of the award-winning architects of the building itself!

Away from the man-made elements of Slimbridge, the designs of some of the birds and ducks themselves are fabulous and extraordinary. They must be inspirational to textile designers and artists. Every colour imaginable, such beauty carried so unself-consciously. You don't need to be an ornithologist to appreciate these miraculously dressed feathered creatures. Which I do for the next two hours, wandering around the ponds and lakes in the hot sunshine, awestruck at their designer's creativity and imagination!

By the time I get back to the hostel, it is bustling with twelve elderly hikers who have arrived for their annual holiday. Apparently it is thanks to them that I can stay there tonight, the hostel normally being shut on a Friday for the autumn season, except for

groups. This evening I share the kitchen and dining room and am offered some of their dinner - and home-made wine! I rather gingerly accept a glass of peapod, but it's delicious. The wine-maker tells me it's the cheapest possible wine to make. I believe him. He says that he and his wife eat the peas, then process the pods into a vintage. There's not much he doesn't know about home-made wine making, and has made wine for years, from everything you can possibly imagine.

After dinner, they generously include me in their sociable evening chatting in the lounge. I learn that they are on their way to Exeter where they start their walking. They have been staying in youth hostels for years and know the ropes intimately.

It's been a fantastic day and more relaxing than the two previous days' cycling when I clocked up over 90 miles. Again I have a dormitory to myself which is real luxury considering it only costs me £10.50 for the night.

I didn't know until yesterday that the Sharpness Canal runs into Gloucester. I feel quite smug at this news since, in anticipation of some canalside rides (most desirable as I know they will be on the flat), I have obtained the required permission for cyclists from British Waterways. This costs nothing and one does not have to prove oneself a worthy citizen. You just have to have this bit of paper dangling from your bicycle if you cycle along one of their towpaths. Why? I wonder.

Walking or cycling along towpaths is a very pleasant experience. The lack of hills aside, they are free from traffic, quiet and often very beautiful. A canal can also take you straight into the heart of a city through the back arteries without having to endure miles of suburban bungaloidal growth. Where I live, the towpath close to my home takes me straight to the supermarket! The bridges and locks have been restored in the spirit of their original robust engineering over the last 20 years or so, thankfully without being over-prettified. And alongside this restoration many of the formerly closed towpaths have been re-opened, allowing greater access to the public. It would be nice, I muse, if the lock-keepers' cottages could once again be occupied by lock-keepers to complete the restoration. I don't really know why - it just would.

So it's a towpath ride into Gloucester in the misty morning sunshine, and life could be worse. It's so peaceful and pleasant and self-indulgent to be enjoying these 12 miles so much! But the centre of Gloucester is disappointing. Just the usual High Street shops which make every city and town in the country look the same. A bit of shopping is quickly done, then off on the A417, not a particularly memorable road, to Ledbury, to spend the night in a B&B in a beauty parlour run by the beautician landlady. It's a shame that a facial treatment is not included, but I'll wait until this fresh air life is over before I undergo some serious grooming.

CHAPTER 13 - Leading By Example

The roads have gradually levelled out and are now a very different kettle of fish from Cornwall, and at last I'm cycling more than walking. In the orchards, trees are drooping with ready-to-pluck fruit, reminding me of my plans to create an orchard at our new home, and fields have just been harvested of potatoes. This area even has vineyards.

The road winds in and out of three counties all day long – Herefordshire, Worcestershire and Shropshire - before I'm finally in just Shropshire. It's extremely pleasant bowling along in the peace and quiet of another sunny autumn day. The weather lately has been perfect, and it feels settled for the moment. The proposed route for today stays mainly on fairly quiet B roads and there's little chance of having to juggle with juggernauts, which puts me in a very calm and contented mood.

It's not only me who's feeling more relaxed - the past few days have also seen my last pair of reading spectacles loosening up so much I can't keep them on my face unless I tilt my head back - not much good when trying to study the map, at the same time as balancing the bike against me, as well as squashing myself into the hedgerows for safety. Since my face, as well as everything else, is usually running with sweat, the spectacles' descent from my slippery nose onto my slippery chin is becoming faster as they become looser. Action will have to be taken very soon.

Bromyard is another pretty little town with very little evidence of a tourist industry - which makes it even prettier. An opticians in the main street has two women assistants, one of whom bears the spectacles off for minor surgery, while the other, a woman about my age, asks about my journey. She is intrigued that I have no sponsors, and that this trip is just for me. We have a long chat about women of our age doing 'our own thing'. Unlike her, I have had a little practice in my life, of taking time out to do what some people would definitely consider 'selfish'. When my children were in their teens I decided that they were too dependent on me and me on them, so I took a five week 'sabbatical', only to discover that being away from them was no answer - I missed them and wanted to be at home. In a small way, though, that episode foreshadowed this trip. I had always known, deep down, that I needed to strike out on my own, to do what I'm doing now.

But this lady has spent her entire life doing her duty and looking after other people, not even a week off, let alone five. She tells me that when she drove her husband to the hospital a short time ago for an appointment, she was ticked off by a volunteer who told her she was too old to work any more – "You should be retired by now," she was told, "And do some voluntary work, like me!"

She tells me passionately that she doesn't want to do any voluntary work, she wants to do something like I am doing. Not necessarily cycling, but just something for her, and only her.

I feel for her completely. It's very difficult to step away from what other people have come to expect of you, including yourself! It's not just changing your own self-image in doing something completely different, it's also educating your nearest and dearest into accepting the new you.

As I embarked on this journey, I had the wholehearted support of all my family. My sister even had a map that she stuck pins in to plot my journey, but I also knew that there would have been no censure if I'd called it a day, admitted I'd bitten off more than I could chew. I'm not sure how well they understood my need to do this. I don't know if I knew until I was on the road, but it was about escaping my comfort zone, discovering what I was capable of. When I was younger I had longed to escape, yearned to travel, but had always scurried home. In my twenties I joined the Foreign Office and had been posted to Norway, only to throw in the towel after five days. "You could come home and marry me," Will said when I rang to tell him how miserable I was. And so I did, three months later. I have never for a moment regretted it, but I do sometimes wish I'd been braver!

It is particularly difficult for women to move the goalposts. This is not meant to be sexist or misogynistic. It is just that it is normally the wife/mother/woman who - either because of nature or nurture (who on earth really knows?) - finds herself slipping into the mould of domestic carer. There are plenty of exceptions but by their very nature they are exceptions. And domestic caring has limited horizons. For the young woman, breaking the mould means major sacrifices. Margot Fonteyn, in choosing to have two terminations, sacrificed motherhood for her art(1). Nowadays things are slightly more liberal, but on some levels, not much.

It's easy for women to feel they have to justify whatever they do – this lady spending her days in the opticians is the same age as me and at our age we should feel it's actually good enough just to say that we're doing it because we want to! My advice to her is to find at least one person who will give her one hundred and ten percent support in whatever way she chooses to express herself. Because I know that, regardless of my need and determination, unless my family *had* approved wholeheartedly of my trip, it would have been infinitely harder to achieve.

My specs having been restored to full working order, I wish her luck and perseverance, and I profoundly hope that she realises her dream. To do something entirely for herself.

1. Meredith Daneman (2004), *A Life – Margot Fonteyn page(177)*, Viking Penguin

It would be truthful, rather than immodest, to say that she showed excitement in my project, and I felt that she saw it as an inspiration for her. I begin to see myself as a continuum of adventurous women, rather than lagging pathetically behind people like Dervla Murphy and Josie Drew, whose books have inspired me. Everything is relative anyway; what is a life-changing adventure for one person would be a common occurrence for another.

I stay the night in a CTC-recommended B&B on the outskirts of Ludlow. It's a pity I have neither the dress, the lover, nor the inclination for a special meal, since Ludlow is becoming increasingly famous for its restaurants. All its famous food shops are closed by the time I arrive for a look around, and although it's a beautiful and historically famous town, complete with a castle and lovely shops, at 6 pm it, in common with almost every other English town, and in spite of so much fame, seems very dead. What do the youngsters do with themselves, besides vroom vrooming around on their motorbikes? I'm always worried about youth in the evenings, having strong memories of my own boredom in my home town of Bexhill, bursting with the pent-up frustration of youth, and of how close I came to seriously misbehaving. I think all that stopped me was that I wasn't entirely sure what I should do to misbehave!

CHAPTER 14 - Treat Time

In marked contrast to the last Americans I met over a breakfast table, there's an anorexic looking American woman and her husband at breakfast. In the course of an interesting conversation with them over the toast, I learn a valuable tip about planting roses. Apparently if you bury a 6" nail with them it will feed them for years. I didn't know this, and resolve to buy a bag of them for mine. I forget to ask what the nails should be made of!

I'm determined to follow a cross-country route to Shrewsbury, with only the very beginning and end on the A49. My map is quite clear and there appears to be a more or less straightforward route using B and minor roads.

Shrewsbury is the final destination for the first stage of my overall trip. Will, coincidentally, has some business there this week and it will be an excellent town in which to spend a few days combining business with rest. He will then waft me and the bike home in comfort - if we can fit the bike into the car. Shrewsbury also has a railway station which makes the town easily accessible for rejoining my route at a later date, without car.

It's very pleasant cycling along the B road to the T junction with another B road, where I'm supposed to go straight on. But there is no sign of a straight on road. Turning left leads to Craven Arms on the A49, turning right goes towards Much Wenlock, about 15 miles away. I have learnt to study maps much more closely than I used to, searching for any symbol on the page which might give me a tiny clue as to where I'm supposed to go, but this time there isn't one.

I reckon that I have more chance of finding a left-turning minor road if I turn right, so I head for Much Wenlock. The road is peaceful and all is quiet, with just a very occasional car. The first left turn I come to is a dark narrow lane, wooded on either side, rising steeply, with a cul-de-sac sign and also - very bizarrely - a Tourist Information symbol! I know I'm being had, but it *is* going in the right direction, and maybe it is only a cul-de-sac for cars. And anyway, there's such a thing as curiosity.... Ten minutes later, however, after much huffing and puffing up and round a most delightful lane with the most delightful little houses, I do reach a dead end – with, of course, no sign at all of a Tourist Information Office!

It's been an amiable diversion, but one which I could well do without. A mile or so further along I eventually come across the right turning left - if you follow me. This takes me to a one-house village, in front of which is a large garden with a couple strolling about, and their dog who barks at me. Fortunately there's a ditch between him and me, and besides, he's not a French chien, which would have been truly awesomely frightening. His owner assures me he's not dangerous - all dog owners say this as their docile cuddlesome rottweiler bounds up to you baring its teeth. (Anyway, how do dog owners know how their pets behave when they're not around? And parents their children?)

The dog momentarily quietened, I ask the man if I'm on the right road for Ticklerton. He asks where exactly I'm hoping to reach. I tell him Church Stretton via the lanes. "Oh, you'll never find it," he says with a warm chuckle. "One elderly gentleman has been cycling around here for the past ten years and never found it yet. He sometimes pops in for a cup of tea!'" I have to tell him I'm certainly not cycling back the way I've come, and please could he give me clear and concise directions. Which he does, but when I ask him why there seem to be no road signs he tells me they have all been taken down by the locals to confuse the anti-hunting brigade. Well, it may work but it also confuses people like me. "If you get stuck," he says, " just call us."

He was so nice I wouldn't have minded getting stuck, and joining him and his 'elderly gentleman' for a cup of tea!

Judging from the dozens of pheasants I see over the next few miles - in the fields, on the roads, panicking in the hedgerows - the locals enjoy shooting as well as hunting. The Dog Man's instructions are excellent and I bowl along, thoroughly loving the absence of traffic and the beauty of the green rolling hills and vales. At a crossroads I pause for thought and a re-evaluation of the situation. Everything is quiet, no sound or sign of anything but the gentle rustle of mature trees. Which way is the right way? A car comes along, stops, the front passenger winds his window down and sticks his head out: "Are you cycling to John O'Groats?" a voice asks.

"Yes," I reply.

His mouth drops open: "I was only being ironic; it's something I've always wanted to do myself."

"Well, it's true, I really am," I tell him, "and I can thoroughly recommend it."
A long conversation ensues, with two silent ladies in the back seat smiling benignly and, most importantly, the driver is able to give me further directions.

Church Stretton is yet another congenial little town with antique shops and a branch railway station. A stop for an ice-cream and rest in the shade - it's hot thirsty work that I'm doing! - and then the final few miles into Shrewsbury along flat country lanes. To get to them I have to cycle about a mile southwards along the A49, into the wind, before turning off. This, happily, is my first experience of the reason one follows a south to north route. Just a mile cycling into a headwind proves that it's the only reason there needs to be.

Shropshire's topography is extraordinary. Small, very steep hills suddenly rise out of plains, hills over which I really don't want to cycle. By a mixture of cunning and luck I manage to avoid these devilish little killers, and I am relieved.

Shrewsbury itself, unlike Exeter, has an excellent cycle-path network, and I soon find myself in the Tourist Information Office trying to find somewhere to sleep. I sit on the steps and phone around, rather hopelessly after a while as the replies are all negative. For want of a better idea, I drift around the town, knocking on doors of inns and B&Bs, all without success. The town is full. The shops are beginning to shut and the previous hustle and bustle is lessening. I imagine myself sleeping on a street bench, being attacked by hoodlums, carted off by the police as a vagrant, dying of hypothermia. How ignominious. How ironic on the last day of this part of my trip. A woman is sweeping the floor of her giftie shop and I ask her if she knows of a place to stay. She looks the sort of person who would know 'nice' places, and she mentions one, nearby. It's trendy, and rather expensive, but after 404 miles, it's my last day of cycling until the next time, and high time to treat myself to a little luxury.

PART II

CHAPTER 1 - On The Road Again

I arrive at Shrewsbury station roughly eight months later at 3 o'clock in the afternoon, with very mixed feelings. Apart from the occasional foray to the supermarket I've done absolutely no real cycling since I left this town in September. Though these outings did provide me with inspiration when, on a couple of occasions I exchanged a few words over the cycle racks with an elderly man, a great-grandfather no less, called Dick, who cycles six miles every day of the week, rain or shine, except Sundays.

I know that it would be easy for me not to do it, to accept people's assurances that I'd done jolly well to have got so far and let that be enough. But I also know that I can't be free in my head until I've completed the entire journey. Stopping now would be to leave something undone, something that would always be there, nagging at me, preventing me from concentrating on the next chapter, the new orchard and vegetable garden, the grandchildren and all the other adventures still to come.

Anyway, here we go again, I think, as I cycle rather gingerly out of the town and into the countryside, with willow wisps of cotton wool blowing in my face. This time, however, I am better equipped, thanks to Will and some very practical birthday presents. I now have panniers that unclip easily, a lightweight, zippable, long sleeved cardigan affair for warmth, and a lightweight waterproof jacket, both made with modern materials that dry quickly. The cardigan affair in particular is in a soft, tactile cosy material, and becomes my comfort rag as I wear it nearly all the time. And since plain water was inadequate in the hot weather of September, I also have a large tin of rehydrating powder which, when mixed with water, replenishes all the minerals and enzymes one loses in sweat. I have had to be persuaded to take this – with space at a premium it's just so big!

I am better equipped physically for the ride to John O'Groats, but mentally it proves much more difficult to get going.

While nurturing the remainder of the journey in my mind over winter, I have fallen into an assumption that I will return home after reaching Glasgow, then continue a few weeks later for the final stage. But a few days ago I changed my thinking and have decided that if I reach the same latitude as Glasgow (which I shall by-pass to the west) within a fortnight, I shall continue on until journey's end. It all depends on how long it takes to reach Largs, which is on the coast, just south of the latitude of Glasgow.

Heat will probably not be a problem this time. Although it is glorious at Watford Station as I set off, by the time I arrive in Shrewsbury the sun has long disappeared and a cold wind has sprung up. But the countryside looks lush and hearty, with cow parsley, hawthorn and lilac in their prime. But not having started today's 19-mile ride until three in the afternoon I am worried that I've set myself too much of a task for my first day.

As I did back in September, I have pre-booked my first night, in a B&B in Whitchurch. On the outskirts of the town a sign indicates a canal nearby, and I make a mental note to find out more about it tomorrow. The 19 miles, as it turns out, have been flat and easy. Needless worry, as always, comes too easily. My landlady for tonight, Mrs G, turns out to be a very spry lady of 75 who, in spite of my objections, grasps the heaviest end of the bike, and helps me haul it up the steps and into the shed, and then launches upstairs with one of my panniers, with me puffing after. Her beautiful Bernese mountain dog called Amber has an intimidating bark and bulk and thoroughly gets in the way, but once the initial excitement of a new smell in the house has worn off, she is a most gentle and well trained animal who endears herself almost immediately. Would that all dogs were like Amber.

The next morning I discover why Amber is such a pleasure to have around, when Mrs G tells me she used to be a trainer of alsatian dogs. Mrs G is so diminutive that the thought of her actually training these magnificent beasts...it would have been fascinating to watch. I think of alsatians as kings of the dog world but am under the impression that they can be unpredictable, and therefore treat them with the utmost wary caution. Mrs G's late husband clearly felt the same and was none too keen on all those alsatians and persuaded her to swap them for Bernese mountain dogs, which she did, and they have been with her ever since.

During the course of the evening, which the three of us spend together in her living room, Mrs G tells me about a very serious operation she had undergone last year - they had only operated on her at all because of her feisty attitude. They had presumptuously decided she was a gonner, but she impressed a junior consultant sufficiently for him to take a bit more time for a proper examination, after which he successfully persuaded a senior consultant that she was, after all, operable. While I eat my salad supper brought from home, we watch a TV programme on hospital food and tut tut in companionable indignation at all the dreadful goings on in the kitchens. It makes me think of Nicholas Culpeper's saying - "A good cook is half a physician." Perhaps someone needs to point this out to the NHS?

Mrs G entertains me with tales of other guests she's had over the years. She particularly admires the way one Australian couple knew how to get about. On arriving by car in a city with expensive parking meters, they would park their car in a hotel car park, go inside for a cup of coffee, then leave the receipt on the dashboard in a prominent position and go and do their sightseeing.

In an old country magazine by my bedside is an article which states that the number of young produced by any creature at a birth is in inverse ratio to the life expectation of the species. I find this fascinating, and spend some time trying to think of a creature who will confound this truth. But it's just a diversion and the final thought of the day is that I feel flat, and wonder if I really want to do this trip after all.

In this mood, my departure next morning is a very reluctant one. I wish Mrs G the best of health and leave her warm and welcoming home with little enthusiasm for the task ahead.

CHAPTER 2 - No Room At The Inn … Again

I now have to find my way to the Shropshire Union Canal which, although signposted on the way in to Whitchurch, is not referred to anywhere else, even in the centre of the town. The Tourist Information Office is not at all informative but various passers-by tell me that Grindley Brook is the nearest point at which one can join it. After various wrong turnings and cross words aired to the ether, I arrive there eventually and I'm told by the lady who runs the small shop that it's called, disconcertingly, the Llangollen Canal. Naturally, she doesn't know whether it's fit for cyclists or not so I take my chance and set off. At first there are plenty of walkers and boats tootling their slow way up and down the canal, but after a while there's an eerie silence and a feeling of aloneness that makes me feel uneasy. Anyway, the towpath surface eventually becomes so difficult to cycle on that after only six miles I have to retrace the last half mile to the road again. It's disappointing as the map shows the canal meandering, admittedly rather circuitously, roughly northwards, but if I hadn't tried it I would not have known that I couldn't do it!

As a compensation, the road through Marbury and Wrenbury runs close to the canal, crossing and re-crossing it several times. Just outside Nantwich I stop for a bowl of celery soup at a pub and then it's the Nantwich by-pass itself until it meets the B5074 to Middlewich. Due to an error in the map-reading department I get to Middlewich via Winsford, which is a completely unrewarding experience. My irritation is compounded by the fact that no pub, B&B or guest house in Middlewich has any rooms this Friday as there seem to be about six weddings in town this weekend and everybody is 'complet'.

A shop assistant mentions a guest house on the outskirts which I passed about half an hour ago, so I trudge back and ring the front door bell. It's a large Victorian house, but with absolutely no sign of life. Nobody answers the door. Feeling a trifle desperate, I use my mobile to call directory enquiries for the phone number of the guest house outside which I'm standing, and find myself in the absurd situation of trying to have a conversation with a woman on the other side of the door. I tell her I'm about three feet away from her, but she makes no attempt to open up. I think she says she is full up but it's almost impossible to hear her as the traffic is so noisy. I wish she had the courtesy to come to the door, or at least to put a sign on her board that she has no vacancies. She starts giving me directions to a place out of town which might have a vacant room but not being able to juggle phone and map and pen with nothing more than a shrub to lean on, and not being able to hear her anyway, I rather abruptly terminate our conversation. She is obviously so successful at her guest house business that she has no need of passing goodwill.

A hotel with the welcome CTC sign outside it is also completely full up with wedding guests, but at least they find me the phone number of a hotel in Holmes Chapel, about five miles away, and their lounge *is* a calm and peaceful place to make a phone call.

When I arrive at the hotel in Holmes Chapel, I learn that it's half price on Friday and Saturday nights so I am in luck, although it's the sort of hotel that I consider incompatible with the spirit of my adventure. Though my journey is not about physical deprivation, I don't want to travel first class. My ride is taking me away from the world of plenty and putting things – physical needs among them – into perspective.

The hotel I'm now booked into is a business establishment which is probably part of a chain. I indulge in a glass of wine in the empty bar, then up to my bland but clean room which looks out onto a fascinating brick wall. A cheese and biscuit supper watching television recharges the batteries, but I have an aching neck and feel somewhat discombobulated.

An enormous breakfast is served to just three guests the following morning, half of which I squirrel away for later. I had planned to travel on the quieter B5081 from Middlewich to Knutsford on the way to Leigh, but because of where I am now I have to settle instead for the A50 which passes through Holmes Chapel.

I have booked a room in advance in a B&B at Leigh, as I'm nervous of venturing into the areas between two such great conurbations as Liverpool and Manchester without a reservation. The CTC route takes as much advantage as possible of the quiet roads which meander in between the two cities, but although I pass many attractive and prosperous looking farmhouses it is not breathtakingly beautiful countryside.

One or other of three motorways, M6, M56 and M62, is never far away, and their distant rumble is audible all day, floating over the erstwhile quiet farmland. Just as I'm thinking it's better than going right through the middle of a major city, I'm shocked to the core to suddenly hear a rottweiler snarling at me with only a fence to stop it tearing me to pieces. Dogs shake me up, the result, I suspect, of living next door, as a child, to an alsatian whose only exercise was running up and down a narrow pen on the other side of our joint garden fence, and whose barking and leaping up to look over at us I can remember to this day. Naturally the dog dazer, another birthday present from Will, who understands my worries about dogs, is packed away inaccessibly, but I do have time to notice in my panic that in fact the fence comprises two fences, both topped with barbed wire. This is obviously to keep strangers out, as well as the dog in, but what is he guarding so assiduously anyway - the Crown Jewels? This happens two or three times today, which I assume is a reflection on this particular area.

I pass from Cheshire into Warrington and finally for today into Greater Manchester, having first crossed a toll bridge over the Manchester Ship Canal near Warburton. The county boundaries are confusing as some of the roads have 'Welcome to the County of X' and some don't and my map doesn't mark any of them. Many fields are lying fallow - the ratio seems to be roughly five to one. What a waste.

I arrive at Leigh mid-afternoon just as the cloud which has been with me since Shrewsbury lifts and the sun arrives to create a beautiful balmy evening. But apart from a quick trip to a local inn by the canal for a salad, I spend the time in my room preparing for a long ride to Slaidburn tomorrow, where I've booked into the youth hostel. From my calculations it would seem to be somewhere between 50 and 60 miles, which is daunting, especially as my neck still aches and so does my bottom. And reading between the lines of the CTC instructions I know that it's going to require some exacting navigation. I rest, watch TV and try to relax.

There's a bath in the bathroom which, with all my aching bones, is just what I need right now to restore myself. But when I lift the non-slip mat to run myself a nice hot bath all the debris and dirt underneath from what looks like several weeks is exposed, and I decide that the thing I most desire in life after all is a shower!

I have to admit to not enjoying myself very much since starting the second leg. Everything is an effort, and I can't understand why my bottom aches this time when it didn't in Cornwall. Then I realise that Cornwall was spent mostly on my feet, walking uphill. I feel I have still not got into my stride, and I am seriously wondering whether I can, or even want to, finish it all the way. I am worried about tomorrow.

LEIGH

HALF WAY TO
LANDS END

HALF WAY TO
JOHN O'GROATS

CHAPTER 3 - Halfway There!

Things look brighter this morning. After my shower yesterday evening, the sun put in a welcome appearance and when I went for a walk and found the canalside pub where I had my supper, my mood lightened slightly. Then my landlady, who is on the CTC list and no stranger to cyclists doing this route, lifts my spirits enormously by telling me that Leigh is the half-way point between Land's End and John O'Groats. I can hardly believe it, but feel encouraged as I cycle through the centre of Leigh - being a Sunday it's peaceful and empty - and the good weather from yesterday evening is carrying through to today. It's beautiful. And miraculously my aches have disappeared.

But I really have to concentrate on the rather cavalier directions which are complicated and mean lots of start/stops for checking and asking and pondering. At one point, after going through Westhoughton, the CTC instructions say: "Turn L on A58, then R in 200 yds sp Lostock. Cross A6, then turn L through Lostock to A58 (Bolton Ring Road). Turn L. At traffic lights with A673 turn R then immediately L..."

These should, more accurately, read: "Turn L on A58, then R in 200 yds which is not signposted. Toil up wide hill which has grass growing out of the tarmac but do not be deterred when, going over the hump of the hill, there appears to be a dead-end of thick shrubbery ahead of you. Look very carefully to your right and you will see a very narrow lane which crosses under the A6. With care cross the slip road and enter the suburbs of what might be Lostock. Take the third turning on your left down a cobbled lane, veering right at the bottom and on up the hill to Lostock Junction, veering right again up through a modern estate to the A58 (Bolton Ring Road)."

By the time I had got to this point, I was so crazed with delight that I was where I was meant to be that instead of turning R at the traffic lights then immediately L, I did just the opposite. Only I couldn't, and quickly, thankfully, discovered my potential mistake.

After this, the road takes me into the hills of Lancashire and through Belmont, where a cyclist joins me companionably while we slog up the hill. He gives me some good advice about the next turning which apparently is quite obscure, and he is in no doubt at all that I will reach Slaidburn this afternoon. His assessment of the remaining mileage is lower than mine, so this is comforting. He tells me he would have ridden a little way with me to make sure that I turned off at the right place but has been held up by mending a puncture for two other girls, and is late for another appointment. A lovely man. I soon find myself having a picnic in the shade of a tree overlooking rolling hills. The only thing to mar the moment is the Sunday motorcyclists, who are out in their dozens, like flies. The lane is a green finger leading directly into

Blackburn, which again is quiet, then it's straight out on the A666 and A59 to Whalley. This is a tourist honey pot where I stop for tea and cake before venturing into the lanes to Slaidburn.

On the map it looks pretty straightforward but once again, the CTC instructions are, to say the least, casual. At Bashall Eaves one should - "Bear L, turn R at *Cow Ark*, up hill and R, then turn L on B6478." A few miles out of Bashall Eaves, with no sign of whatever Cow Ark is, I become seriously concerned that I have, without knowing it, passed it already, and therefore missed the crucial turning, or that I'm just not on the right road, although the sun does seem to be round about in the right place for the direction in which I'm supposed to be going. The thought of turning back is bringing me out in even more of a sweat than the unaccustomed heat is already producing. There's nobody around to ask in these isolated lanes, just the occasional passing car. About five miles out of Bashall Eaves, coming towards me from the other direction is the only person I see to ask, but he's a fully geared up, Lycra-suited, gloved and helmeted, drop handle-barred, head down and pounding out the miles, cyclist, to whom I bawl as we pass each other - "Cow Ark ahead?". Silence. Then, faintly in the distance - "Yes!" Somewhat encouraged by this tenuous assurance that I'm not miles from where I should be, I plough on. Eventually, all of seven miles out of Bashall Eaves, I do just spot the name of Cow Ark, which turns out to be a rather small sign for a house, but to do the CTC instructions justice, it's the only thing around which one could pinpoint as a landmark, other than "big trees". In spite of my anxiety, it has been a fabulously beautiful ride. The sun has shone all day long, Slaidburn is a delightful village, the hostel is very old and full of character, and I have a dormitory to myself. I'm very tired, although the odometer only registers 45 miles, and not the 50-60 I was expecting. It's probably emotional, as much as anything.

I feast on tinned macaroni cheese for supper and, as there's no-one to talk to, I do some washing, remembering a tip that if you wring out your clothes as hard as possible, wrap them as tightly as possible in a towel, then sit on them for five minutes, shake them out and hang them up, they will be dry by morning.

I go to bed with trepidation about the steepness of the hills and loneliness of the moors to come, feeling very tired, saddle-sore, flat, miserable and losing the will to live.

I must eat better.

CHAPTER 4 - A Nice Cup Of Tea

My clothes have dried! And it's cloudy with a north-west wind. Three other cyclists in the hostel are preparing to cycle back to their homes after their weekend away, and I envy them knowing where they are going. Because I don't.

I would like to have stayed at Dent youth hostel on the edge of the Yorkshire Dales but I haven't booked the required 48 hours ahead. I had also planned to cross the moors to High Bentham to get there, but one of this morning's cyclists advises me against it - lots of confusing side roads on which it would be all too easy to go wrong, lots of very steep ups and downs and lots of lonely moors stretching in all directions. I opt instead to stick to the B road I'm already on and to make for Settle via Tosside.

Tosside, when I reach it, seems to be the centre of the building trade. Scaffolding, lorries and materials piled up everywhere. At first glance it seems there's nothing much here to stop for but - there is a sign for refreshments. I can only see a Post Office though, which is combined with a very small general store and as I need stamps I push the door. It's locked. A notice says that should the shop be locked during opening hours, to ring the bell. Which I do. And a young man crosses the yard with some keys and lets me in. He sells me stamps and I ask where is the café? This is it, he says, I shall bring you some tea. He brings two mugs and I settle myself comfortably on one of the two chairs which are the café, and we talk about cycling. His brother and a friend have done this ride in four days for charity. That is no mean feat; it really is fantastically fast. He says that the old pub being given a face lift on this side of the village is in Lancashire; where the new building is going up on the other side of the village is North Yorkshire. It's going to be the village hall. Hence all the building debris. It is literally a border village. We have a satisfying chat in these very modest surroundings and I feel happier than I have done for some time. I have always felt at home in Yorkshire, which is my father's county. Maybe the fact that Will's an architect means all the builders' mess makes me feel at home!

It's a rural ride from Tosside to Settle, with somnambulant sheep and lambs half hidden in fields of buttercups, and bluebells and wild garlic littering the hedgerows. Wonderful.

I eat a good lunch in a Settle café and call in at the Tourist Information Office to find somewhere to stay in Ingleton. I feel reluctant to just launch myself into the unknown in this area without somewhere to aim for. At vast expense £1.50 - they book me into one of Ingleton's pubs, the B&Bs on their list being full. Ingleton is just off the A65 and I have pleasant memories of driving in the other direction down this road in the 80's, listening to Nigel Lawson unfolding one of his budgets while I enjoyed being practically the only driver on this beautiful road. Alas, I think, as I'm buffeted by the cross draught from countless lorries and cars, those days are long gone. The first thing I see as I enter Ingleton is a row of three B&Bs all advertising vacancies! I check the price of one and it's half the price of the pub, so I book in there and then. This is my first inkling that perhaps Tourist Information Offices exist more to sell souvenirs than to be helpful.

The first thing I do is ring to cancel my room with the pub, then to have a look around the town which is dominated by a magnificent viaduct. This used to carry thousands of railway passengers a year to enjoy the Waterfalls Walk which is apparently, "4.5 miles of everchanging waterfalls and woodland scenery with breathtaking views around every corner..." It must be a must to visit. Ingleton itself is a good base for holidaying - on the edge both of the Yorkshire Dales and the Lake District. One day I shall come back here and do the tourist thing in greater comfort.

In spite of its apparent sophistication though, the town only seems to have one restaurant, which is shut. At the pub it is steak night tonight and, fool that I am, I think it's bound to be good. Unfortunately, it is thin and tough, the onion rings are mainly soggy batter, the salad is watery and the chips cold. It's not just me that is dissatisfied; the couple at the next table, I am glad to hear, also complain. Rather than sustaining life, which food should do, this positively endangers it - or at least, one's enjoyment of it.

There is a good mobile phone signal from here, which there wasn't from Settle, and I have a long chat with Will who cannot believe I have come so far. I remind him that while everybody else in my life is earning their living, I am spending at least six to seven hours a day just pedalling. After this I book myself in at a B&B in Tebay for tomorrow, and fall asleep feeling much happier. It was the Tosside mug of tea and builders' mess which did it!

Despite the horrid meal last night I am in a much more cheerful frame of mind this morning.

At breakfast the landlord mentions his interest in my bike, which he's had a good look at in his garage. It has a very good ratio between the chain wheel and rear sprocket he says. Sensing my struggle to make an intelligent response, he expands his remark. It means, he says, that when you are going uphill you have low gears and when you are going downhill you have high gears, so you can do both! Ah. Don't all bikes have this ability, then? Apparently not. I now regard my derailleur gears with a bit more respect - and use them a bit more intelligently.

I plan to get to Tebay via Sedburgh on the A683. Kirkby Lonsdale is by-passed by cutting a corner near Cowan Bridge which is an attractive place to stop for a drink. The old stone bridge spans a large river whose waters look very low, considering this is early summer.

For the next hour or so I cycle along a quiet road wending its way between hills looking smooth and clean-shaven. The wind is cold but the sun comes out occasionally to warm me up. I think I've got a slight chill on my tummy as from time to time I feel gripes and I'm sure it's because this cold wind has been around for days. At Sedburgh I buy a quiche for supper and have a bowl of hot soup sitting in a hot corner of a pub yard. A couple nearby have two dogs which they solicitously fuss over. They are abandoned strays from the RSPCA. One is a lurcher-cross I'm told - a breed I've never heard of - which I refer to as an elderly 'he'. But I'm told it's a young she. I suggest rather facetiously that she has electrolysis to remove her whiskers but her owners don't appreciate my joke.

Perhaps they didn't hear it! The peace was intermittently shattered with Sedbergh 'enjoying' the sight –and sound – of frequent RAF manoeuvres above our heads.

Just outside Sedbergh I join a quiet road, the B6257, which goes under the M6 to join the A685 which then goes over the motorway again before it reaches Tebay. From now until north of Carlisle my route will never take me far from the motorway, and even if I can't see it, I will certainly be able to hear it. I have noticed that motorway noise extends far into the quiet countryside, so that complete silence is impossible to find. Even bird song sounds loud and it's been discovered that sometimes they sing louder to make themselves heard!

I have been told that Mrs Jones, my landlady for tonight, will be out when I arrive but have been given instructions. There is a notice hoping visitors will take advantage of the garden, which I do, and settle down with my maps, notebook and a cup of tea in a wind-free sunny spot, noticing that the hot soup must have settled my tummy as the gripes have gone away. An hour or so later Mrs Jones appears and gives me a warm welcome. Her dog is with her, by chance looking exactly the same as the one at lunchtime. Is she a lurcher-cross I ask knowledgeably? It's a 'he' I'm informed. Another one who looks ancient. I think it's the arthritic way they move which gives them the appearance of age. Slowly and carefully as if trying to arrange their limbs in as comfortable a position as possible.

CHAPTER 5 - Just Like In The Movies

After an excellent and very friendly breakfast I set off in the direction of the attractive village of Orton, which has a chocolate factory and a regular farmers' market. Unfortunately, the latter doesn't happen on Wednesdays and half past nine is too early to stop at the former for a mug of hot chocolate. It's a small family enterprise which obviously manages to keep going in spite of the mountain of brain-deadening paperwork which is required these days simply to sell a teaspoon. Another place to put on the list for a vist in the future.

The next village, Shap, hoves into view round about elevenses time but instead of being another Orton where it would be a pleasure to stop for a drink, it's bereft of chocolate factories or cafés, so I just keep going in the drizzle. The road has now joined the A6 which goes all the way into Carlisle.

At Penrith I buy an Emergency Bag (otherwise known as a turkey roaster). Should one inadvertently have to spend a night outside, this bag will keep one alive, insulated and warmed by one's own body heat.

It would be very inadvertent, but I feel more secure carrying one just in case. It's made of a lightweight foil-like material and is the same as that which is wrapped around marathon runners when they've finished running. It's one of the magical spin-offs from the NASA space development programme.

After Penrith, it's out onto the moors again, where a baby rabbit is startled, tries to run away, but keeps falling over on to his back. It isn't just panic, something is obviously very wrong. His legs are not bloodied as they would be if he'd escaped from a trap, and it doesn't look like myxomatosis. Someone, when I recount the incident later, says that it could be a genetic fault. But it's awful to watch.

There are cowslips, poppies, and a group of oyster catchers, with their squeaky call. Oyster catchers on the moors? There will be a lot of them in the days to come, but these are the first. And yet another RAF plane - at least I assume it's one of ours! - practising low level flying.

It's a fairly straight run into Carlisle. It wouldn't be quite fair to say that it doesn't acknowledge the cyclist, but it's not much more than a nod and a wink. The cycle lanes are just about wide enough to accommodate a wheel, and require the utmost concentration to keep within them. It's quite a challenge and I feel like a highwire trapeze unicyclist.

On the outskirts of Carlisle I ring a B&B which advertises itself in a tourist brochure. They can put me up, but apparently it's too complicated to explain how to get to them so the proprietor will meet me at the railway station wearing a check shirt and driving a black Mercedes. This is Bond movie stuff. We both arrive at the rendezvous at the appointed time, make discreet eye contact, then he leads me unobtrusively to the safe house. Once there, I am quickly shown the back gate entrance off a quiet and lonely alleyway, given brief instructions as to security, then left alone to send messages to my own special contacts to reassure them that all is going according to plan. I spend the evening out of sight behind curtains, planning tomorrow's incursion into Scotland.

In reality, the B&B is an elegant house in a conservation area; the proprietor is a historian and there are lots of interesting things around, giving it an air of faded gentility. The evening is spent resting quietly after the excitement of being in a Bond movie and a circus in the course of a single day. I want to try out the turkey roaster!

CHAPTER 6 - Another Country

This is going to be a significant day. Goodbye England, hallo Scotland.

The A74 would be the most straightforward route to Gretna Green out of Carslisle but even the brave CTC cyclists recommend the A7 to Longtown, then the A6071 westwards. It means two sides of a triangle rather than one, but safety is paramount.

I have to take the usual photo of The First and Last House in Scotland, and also feel a stop at Gretna Green is obligatory, tourist spot though it is. The souvenir shop, however, is stunningly tempting, with beautifully packaged food, top quality clothes, albeit a bit Princess Anne'ish, and an inexhaustible variety of whiskies. It's a good thing my carrying capacity is restricted. But I do buy a spurtle from the woodturner, just for its name. A spurtle is a porridge stirrer and is nothing more than a long tapered piece of wood, with some fancy carving on the end to hold it by. It's supposed to be easier to clean than a wooden spoon, as porridge is glutinous and sticks to everything. A chopstick would do just as well, or even the handle of a wooden spoon, but whatever its function, a spurtle is an absolute must!

GRETNA GREEN

It's an uneventful ride along the B724, a flat quiet road to Cummertrees, where I have booked into a B&B. Roger and Helen are the proprietors, and their house is one of a unique terrace of late Victorian houses which were built as part of a project to develop the Solway coast into a Blackpool of the North. For various reasons, including, so I'm told, treachery, betrayal and general improbity the scheme was never completed, and these architectural gems stand alone and rather bizarrely with their lovely balconies and interesting elevations.

I arrive slightly earlier than arranged but I am nevertheless given a cordial welcome and shown to my room - called the Tart's Room - and I am also shown the other guest room. The windows and beds of both rooms, plus the tables and chairs, are covered with gorgeous and sumptuous materials, enough to keep Sandersons going for years Large generous swathes of folded and pleated floral patterned fabric cover the windows, while the bed has a fabulous canopy dripping with more material lined with frilly netting and furbelows, and piled high with similarly treated pillows. The character of both rooms is splendidly over the top and theatrical. What a contrast to the antiseptic, primly correct places which nevertheless boast umpteen awards for this and that - all quite meaningless since they don't measure conviviality (*the* most important ingredient in the recipe) - and which, quite frankly, threaten one's will to live. Clearly this place has been created by a couple who love life and meeting people and giving pleasure. But let's not mention the spring cleaning!

After a short rest, enjoying the glorious comfort of my room for a while, and as the sky is clearing, a walk is called for. Roger and Helen advise making for the Solway Firth, along the side of the golf course. They suggest calling in at the hotel bar for a glass of wine, which I do and take it out to the sand dunes overlooking the Firth towards Skiddaw in England. It's a lovely view. A couple of boys are pootling around on their bikes, seemingly content just to be out in the fresh air in a quiet part of a quiet village on a quiet evening in the sunshine, overlooking the sea. The three of us are the only people around. This is the site of the northernmost colony of Natterjack Toads but it's too early in the evening for their appearance - or rather sounds - as they are too elusive to catch sight of. There is still a chilly breeze, but the sky looks clearer by the minute and it augurs well for tomorrow. Well, hope springs eternal ...

Strolling amongst the reddy-brown muddy sandbanks I spy a lost golf ball looking like a miniature nuclear fast reactor just rising from the ground. I keep it as a souvenir of this tranquil evening. Having experienced the simplicity of this little area, I'm rather glad it was not developed into a busy thriving holiday town, although no doubt the employment implications would have been of significance to the locals.

On my return to the B&B Roger introduces me to another guest who invites me to help him finish his bottle of wine. A beautiful crystal wine glass is produced and we settle ourselves into the Louis the Something chairs for conversation. The Other Guest is in the food industry. There have been reports in the paper recently questioning the safety of eating farmed salmon, and other reports criticising these reports, so it's difficult, if not impossible, to get to the objective truth. It seems nonsense to eat farmed salmon to keep one's heart healthy, only to get cancer instead. According to him, farmed salmon is no more dangerous to eat than wild, whose diet is not rigorously controlled as is that of the farmed fish. The diet of the latter is made up of pellet food made from fish from the Pacific Ocean, which is not so polluted as northern seas, which is where the wild salmon feed. His explanation is too simplistic, too convenient. What about the ethics, and sustainability, of catching healthy fish in the southern hemisphere to feed farmed fish in the northern hemisphere, because northerners have permitted their own waters to become polluted?

As far as supermarkets are concerned, I'm told, we should have a certain sympathy for them, as the health and safety regulations they are obliged to follow are so rigorous the food can easily lose everything which makes it worth eating. All the same - sympathy...? My sympathy is in inverse proportion to their profit margins. There is a madness afoot. We've most of us, I imagine, scoffed at labels on packets of nuts which say that the contents may contain nuts! Pre-washed, packeted lettuce is dunked in chlorine 20 times stronger than swimming pool water and the packets themselves treated to keep the lettuce 'fresh'. Have we lost the skills necessary to wash lettuce? And why do people buy 'Easy Cook Rice' which has no doubt been processed by some dubious Frankenstein method and is more expensive than the ordinary stuff which you just throw into a pan of boiling water? But it's not just food labelling which is a nonsense. A new pack of playing cards I bought recently had this legend printed on its side 'The contents of this pack may vary'!

Roger has asked if he can take a photo of me and bike outside the house tomorrow morning, to put on their website. This is so-o-o flattering. An early night, for beauty sleep in my luxurious bordello bed!

CHAPTER 7 - In Front Of The Camera

So - a photo shoot! After the appointment with the hairdresser (comb), the make-up girl (lipstick), wardrobe (scarf), props (bike), I am ready to meet the photographer (Roger) on location (on pavement, outside their house). Such is the miracle of modern (obscene!) technology that by this evening my picture will be on his website, so that my family can see at their get-together for Beccy's birthday that I'm still alive and relatively in one piece. His website covers the whole county of Dumfries and Galloway; as the official one is so inadequate he's done one himself. It would seem to be an undiscovered county with wonderful lakes and forests that nobody knows about...my appetite to explore more of this Scottish county has been whetted, and I am definitely going to come back to this unspoilt corner of Britain, and next time will sample some of Helen's delicious sounding cooking.

My hosts are unhappy that I'm setting off along the A76 to Kilmarnock without a booking for tonight, so at the last minute I make one at a guest house in Thornhill, mainly to set their minds at rest but also in the event, to do the same for myself. Sometimes I just feel too lazy to do anything about it. It's cold and raining as I set off, continuing on the B724 through Dumfries, where I join the A76. The terrain is mostly flat, with surrounding hills coming and going, first near then further away, but ever-changing. I pass a Museum of Banking, which intrigues me, but there's no time to stop. Although, as it happens, I could have done as I arrive too early for the guest house, whose name I found in a tourist brochure. Although I've booked a room here, I knew there was a possibility that I would arrive earlier than I would have liked to stop, so I have made some enquiries along the way. A lady in a tea house by the side of the road earlier, where I enjoyed an enormous slice of home-made sponge and cream, assured me that, absolutely yes, there are lots of B&Bs between Thornhill and Sanqhar - the next little town along.

But, having arrived at Thornhill and before continuing onwards, I need confirmation of this. The Community Office lady on the outskirts of Thornhill does her best to find out for me if there's any likelihood of more B&Bs along this road, and after numerous phone calls we come to the conclusion the answer is negative. Sanqhar is 14 miles further on and yet another lady, this time in the bookshop in Thornhill, agrees with the Community Office lady and disagrees with the Sponge Lady. "You'll be better off staying in Thornhill", she says, "as there's nothing between here and New Cumnock (23 miles away), and you won't want to stay there - it's not a nice place"! As some very dark clouds are beginning to gather, it's getting on for five o'clock and there's no consensus, I lose my nerve about going on this afternoon and I honour my reservation by presenting myself at the B&B. A notice on the door requests guests to report to the George Hotel - on the High Street a short distance away - which I do. However, the reception at the George is shrouded in a gloomy unlit twilight - empty to boot - with another notice saying that if reception is unattended to ring the bell in the public bar through the swing doors. Feeling as though I'm on a treasure hunt of dubious reward I continue my quest, only to find said doors locked. All these instructions are irritating, and unwelcoming. But a young man appears who informs me that the guest house is now manned - or womanned, as it turns out.

I trot back, sighing with martrydom, to the guest house, where I check in with the proprietress. The price seems to be £2 more than is quoted in the brochure. When I mention this triviality, I am told that I have been given an outdated brochure by the Gretna Green Tourist Office. This cannot be true as I saw the very same one in the Dumfries Tourist Office. I mention this too, but I am informed politely that I am free to go elsewhere if I wish - but I know, and she knows, and I know that she knows, there's nowhere else in Thornhill with vacancies for tonight. I have to concede, but am cheered up when I'm shown my room. It is very stylish. Style is obviously the priority ingredient here, with a spacious 'wet room',and beautiful linen on the bed. My soul has been bought for a touch of style - at least for tonight..

But I quietly mourn the passing of the old-fashioned, friendly little farmhouses that one used to find everywhere in the countryside.

The atmosphere in the guest house is also very modern and minimal, but cold, and silence is king. Breakfast does not live up to the promise offered by the beautiful china. The service is so solicitous that the tea is poured out for me and I'm only just allowed to lift the cup to my lips myself, but it doesn't make up for the fact that the Loch Fyne kipper is overboiled, curled up and is only half a kipper anyway. The only other couple in the dining room is French. It's places like this which make me feel lonely, on the rare occasions that I do. I have to resist the urge to put the napkin on my head and dance a jig.

Behind the small linear towns along the A76 there is virtually nothing to be seen except green, lush countryside, so it's amusing to see a sign for 'Get Ahead Hats' pointing up a tiny lane, a few miles outside Thornhill. A little further on there's a most beautiful gorge with designated picnic spot, ideal for a ten-minute break, just to relax in the sunshine and enjoy the setting. The river has an arctic sparkle but, after the emotional coolness of last night's stopover, the sunshine warms my spirits as much as my body,. The plan for today is to get to Kilmarnock where there are bound to be B&B's lining the road in, just as there were at Carlisle. I'm hoping the A76 won't be too heavy with traffic, but if it is I will just have to cope as there's no alternative route.

Sanquar turns out to have four B&B's, all looking decent and inviting! Ha! I cycle on through New Cumnock, which has the most fabulous mural on a pub wall, stopping just before its outskirts for a simple picnic lunch in a field. I continue through Cumnock, halting in a tiny café in Mauchline for a cup of tea and a short rest. I'm fatigued, not by the cycling which has been relatively easy and uneventful today, but by the constant noise of cars passing. I've been on the A road all day, and all day they have been zooming past me at regular intervals, and it's been horrible. I sip my tea and observe people coming into Mick's Café; it takes a while in my present zombie mode to realise they are coming in for a particular reason - home-made ice-cream! Which of course I must experience.

This refreshes me for the final push to Kilmarnock. It's about five in the afternoon when I reach it, and the shops are beginning to shut. I sail into town with complete confidence, *knowing* there will be a vast selection of B&B's to choose from, looking forward to my evening's rest. Except...there is not a single one in sight. I am tired, hot and dusty, and do not know what to do!

ARCHIE THE FARMER'S
LIMOUSINE BULLS

CHAPTER 8 - Third Time Lucky

The only person in sight is a young man with a rucksack on his back. Because of the rucksack, I think he's a traveller and will know of places to stay! As it happens, he doesn't, apart from one which used to operate a few streets away, a long time ago. There's no reply when I ring the bell, but I see a man doing things to his car in his driveway. On being asked for likely places to stay, he says he doesn't know the area very well, but his girlfriend might know somewhere. He fetches her, and she says that she has a friend who used to do guests but she has not spoken to her for two years. But she will phone her, adding that I could have stayed with them if her daughter had not come home for the weekend. I feel somewhat embarrassed at her kind suggestion, but reassure her that that wouldn't have done at all, without meaning a word of it. They seem a very nice couple and I would not have minded at all staying there! She disappears for about 20 minutes, reappearing eventually with a bit of paper with three phone numbers on it. Her friend says every room in Kilmarnock is taken for the weekend because a certain entertainer is in town! She's taken so long on the phone because she and her friend had a lot of catching up to do! I settle myself on their brick wall in the sunshine with my mobile and the list, while the man hovers helpfully, doing inexplicable things to his car.

I feel very tired indeed, and after a long day's riding do not feel in the least like having to work hard to find a bed. I'm beginning to seriously doubt my sanity. The first two places I ring are booked up - there's a dog show on tomorrow as well. I'm becoming slightly flushed, with anxiety and embarrassment as well as the sun, as I dial the final number. I don't like the fact that I might be a worry to this solicitous couple if I have to cycle away without a resolution, as well as a big worry to myself, but mercifully, the third and final phone call yields a positive result. A cheerful male Scots voice gives me instructions on how to find the farmhouse, five miles away in Kilmaurs - and adds that the kettle is on already!

The voice belongs to Archie, a farmer of Limousine bulls, and as I cycle into view about half an hour later he's sitting in his front garden to make sure I don't just sail on by! I am exceedingly pleased to see his smiling face and am quickly shown my room by his wife Agnes, then ushered into their living room for a cup of tea and cakes. I am rather abashed to be told that last year a 57-year-old woman had stayed with them also on her way to John O'Groats, and she had written to them on completion of her End-to-End after only 24 days of cycling. This is excellent timing and I feel jealous.

Another guest staying here is a mechanic called Paul who works for a local fun fair. He's off to Irvine for supper and I ask him if he would mind if I joined him. He says he would welcome company and, as he's been staying in the area for more than a month already, I'm more than happy to let him choose where we eat, not having much faith that anywhere will meet with my food approval! We travel in his van and Paul decides on the Ship Inn for this evening's refuelling. I notice a sign in its window saying that they don't serve children's special menus, that they can have smaller portions of adult food, and they don't serve chips. I love this philosophy and when I am served the most succulent lamb shank, smooth mashed potatoes with a lovely rich gravy and lots of steamed vegetables, I can quite see why the pub is bursting at the seams. It is a most delicious meal and I wish it were my local. Paul is good company, except I don't understand a word of his Northumbrian accent. I refer to it as a Geordie accent, but he tells me that a Geordie accent is spoken only by someone from Newcastle, not the rest of Northumberland. I stand corrected.

Breakfast is companionable, with Archie and Agnes providing an entertaining double act, as well as a wonderfully sustaining meal. All too soon I have to leave their friendly home. They wish me luck as I leave them. They have provided an oasis to a weary, hot and anxious traveller. But at least I know where I'm destined for today - a Blue Hostel in Largs. The Blue Hostels list comprises dozens of private hostels in Scotland and the list is distributed by the Tourist Information Offices. There are many more of them than those belonging to the YHA, so between the two I hope I shall not have to stay at too many B&Bs, which are always more expensive. Largs is also where I have to decide whether to complete the journey in one go or have a rest for a few weeks before continuing. Being well within the fortnight I set myself to reach here, it looks like I shall just go on.

Diverting to Kilmaurs yesterday means I have had to go slightly out of my intended way to Irvine, but it's more pleasant. I join the A737 at Kilwinning and round about a decent time for elevenses there is a sign to Dalgarven Mill. The quiet and narrow lane leading to it descends down a slight incline and round a corner, and immediately one enters the Victorian rural industrial age. There's a bucolic abandon to the hedgerows, and a rusting old plough is quietly ending its days half hidden in the undergrowth. Through the lush greenery of large old trees I get a glimpse of the grey stone walls of the mill, and there's an intimate cluster of cottages, an antique shop, a small courtyard and the mill itself, which houses a café and a costume museum. It's quite magical.

Although the exhibition space in the museum is tiny, there are dozens of costumes, beautifully made and cared for. There are drawers of Ayrshire embroidery and lace, of fans and gloves, the hands which made these exquisite items also being used for the rough farming jobs that women had to do as well. It has all been lovingly and thoughtfully set out. Upstairs, the workings of the mill are explained, although it's not working today. On show are the horse harnesses, churns, tools and machinery used for milling and farming in days long gone, as well as museum pieces of domestic appliances. Although people of the past may have had none of our brutish inventions like the atom bomb or MacDonalds for instance, the museum dramatically brings home how much more physically demanding the everyday chores of existence were then.

The first written evidence of a mill on this site comes from 1573, although it's believed a mill has been here since the fourteenth century. Not this one, of course, which was rebuilt in 1880 - by Sir Bryce Blair of Blair - after a fire destroyed the one from 1640. It seems that a small group of people are involved in keeping this fragment of the past alive for us to learn from and enjoy. It's a pleasure to be here and I rejoin the main road and re-enter the present century reluctantly, attuning my senses to the sights and sounds of modern transport once again.

I continue on the A737 until it joins the B784 where I stop briefly for a picnic lunch. I'm looking for a spot with my back to a quarry and the wind, out of sight of pylons and in sight of the moors, and in the sun. What I find is a spot with my back to the quarry, in the wind, looking out onto pylons, out of the sun. It's a quick lunch. This road joins the A760 just west of Kilbirnie, and is not the best road to cycle on. The wind has now decided to blow from the west, because that's the direction I'm travelling towards of course, and the road surface is badly maintained, bumpy, gravelly, pot-holed and just awful. In fact, the bike is jumping so agitatedly that the mirror can't hold its position which means that I can't see what's behind me. I can't hear anything either, as the wind is so noisy, which means I cannot judge whether it's safe to swerve from potholes. I feel I'm on a trampoline, springing up and down and occasionally catching glimpses of what's on the other side of the stone walls. One Olympic spring, worthy of a gold medal at least, reveals a beautiful view of the Firth of Clyde with Great Cumbrae Island in the distance. It's entrancing - and lifts my mood considerably as I swoop down the one and a half miles of an extraordinarily steep and narrow hill.

CHAPTER 9 - By Any Other Name

The hostel is situated right at the foot of this grand hill, just where it joins the A78 into Largs. I check in straight away. The proprietress admires the fact that I have cycled down "the brae hill". Her admiration would be more justified I think, if I had cycled up it.

Next, a visit to the Tourist Information Office as I urgently need to know where I can book a room for tomorrow. My map shows no habitation between here and Inverary, which is about fifty miles away, and I need reassurance that there is in fact somewhere between here and there to stay. Being a Sunday, with the town bursting with tourists, the Office is naturally shut. But the Largs and Millport Information Bureau is open, and manned by two jolly men who are keen to be helpful. They are astonished to hear that Inverary is fifty miles away, and insist that it's one hundred miles distant, that my map must be wrong, that there are bound to be lots of places to stay along the way, and give me the phone number of Visit Scotland, the official and newly named Scottish Tourist Office. I am invited to phone them, which I do, and then am apologetically charged for the call. Since Scottish tourism has been centralised now, I find I'm ringing someone in Edinburgh who only has a computer to help her find a place somewhere on the A815. She requires a few place names to go by, but this is the problem - there aren't any, which is why I'm phoning her. There is a tiny name - Uig - on my map and I go away armed with all of two phone numbers of B&B's in Uig. The two gentlemen are extremely proud to have been able to help.

Later in the evening I phone one of the B&B's from the hostel and without difficulty get a room for tomorrow. My relief is short-lived, however, and abruptly dispelled when I ask if I need special instructions to find the establishment somewhere near the A815. There's a puzzled silence coming from the other end.

"There's no A815 on the Isle of Skye", the voice says. "That is the Uig you want, isn't it?"

Oh dear! Better to know now, I guess! I have done all I can - if the worst comes to the worst, at least I have the turkey roaster.

I go to sleep reading C P Snow's "The Sleep of Reason", hoping it will help me keep mine, but I don't get beyond the title.

There doesn't seem to have been anybody else staying here last night, but as I prepare my breakfast in the communal kitchen another presence makes itself felt. A woman in black has glided in quietly, smiling serenely. We introduce ourselves. Her name is Barbara Ann and she is from Texas, but has lived in Scotland for several years, working with Together Ministries in Millport.

However, she cannot get a permanent visa to stay here, and every six months she has to leave Scotland for 24 hours in order to renew it. This is not too onerous and she has gone on like this for some time, but it does seem like bureaucratic pomposity. Her air of calmness, she tells me, is misleading! Inside she is a churning mass of tempestuousness. She is sure that she's talking to a celebrity, which warms my ego considerably, but indicates to me that she's lacking a certain grasp on reality!

I depart from Largs, feeling spiritually uplifted by Barbara Ann, and enjoy the next seven or eight miles of flat cycling along the coast road to Gourock, to catch the ferry across the Firth of Clyde to Hunter's Quay near Dunoon. It's cold with a fine drizzle, but it concerns me that it looks much mistier over the water and I wonder if I'll be able to see anything at all of the road on the other side. There's little more enjoyable in life than sailing between Scottish islands in still, calm weather, but today is disappointing because everything is so grey. Looking back from Hunter's Quay, Greenock appears as misty as Hunter's Quay did from Greenock! But the rain is now falling with determined persistence and I promise myself lunch at a place recommended by a woman on the boat - Sheila's Diner - about five miles away.

Hunter's Quay, as I cycle past its outskirts in the rain, looks the bleakest place on earth, and this morning's uplifted spirits have plummeted, even though the road runs alongside Holy Loch! I need a hearty lunch at the diner and order a baked potato, coleslaw and salad. Portions tend to be rather large in Scotland and my plate is overflowing with food, but it's fresh and delicious and it all soon disappears. When I leave I feel like Falstaff having to be hoisted on to his horse, and am sure my saddle will buckle with the extra weight. The rain has finally stopped, the sun even makes the occasional coy appearance and it's a beautiful ride through the Argyll Forest Park. I have plenty of time to appreciate the trees and bluebells. It's good to see the bluebells are the real native ones, *Endymion nonscriptus*, with their delicately drooping flowers looking too heavy for their stems, and not the foreign invader, the upright, more rigid *Endymion hispanicus* (Spanish bluebell), which is becoming more dominant in English woodlands, causing quite a problem south of the border.

Despite the pleasure of the ride though, there is always at the back of my mind the worry that I do not have anywhere to stay tonight, and by the time I reach Strachur after 33 miles I have had enough for today. My chain - or gears - or something - is making a clanking noise, which concerns me a little. It's more than ten miles to the next little black dot on the map, Cairndow, so I must find somewhere here. The Post Office has a B&B sign, but they say their one room is already taken. The only other place is the hotel which looks expensive. However, needs must. The young man on reception says they have a room which he can let me have as a 'deal' as it is free for one night between two long lets. A 'deal' it may be to him, but the price is a great deal to me. However, I have no choice - apart from the turkey roaster - so I will just have to make the best of it. As I puff my way upstairs behind the young man, whose offer to carry my panniers for me was so feeble I felt obliged to refuse, I can't help but think of dear Mrs G, half the size and twice the age of this young man, who didn't bother to ask but just did it.

I have got beyond the feelings of guilt whenever I find myself in more luxurious surroundings than I feel appropriate for this particular journey. And I have also come to realise that the long afternoon rests are as important to the completion of the entire project as is the actual pedalling. So I rest awhile and watch the television. But it's the view which I find so compelling. The sky is slowly clearing although it still wears its habitual unsettled look, and the hills on the further side of the loch look bare and suitably lonely.

I just remember to attend to the bicycle chain before I go into the bar for a drink. All I can do is to wax it, and hope that is sufficient to make the noises go away! I don't know what else to do. On my way to the bar, I notice some books on a table by Fitzroy Maclean. Leafing through them, it slowly dawns on me that this is the very hotel I have wanted to stay in for years, ever since coming across one of Maclean's books on the Caucasus, and learned he owned a hotel in Scotland which had a very good reputation for bonhomie. Not many books are written by members of the British establishment about the Caucasus, which is of particular interest to me in view of my family's connection to it, and Sir Fitzroy Maclean was an acknowledged expert and irresistible travel writer, as well as being a renowned character among hotel-owners. I am exceedingly excited by this discovery, and feel that I am obviously meant to be here! My suspicions are later confirmed by the present owner (Sir Fitzroy Maclean died several years ago).

A bar-propper is holding forth on the subject of herrings in the bar while I sip a glass of wine. I pay little attention to the herring man as I try instead to imagine what it must have been like in Sir Fitzroy Maclean's day.

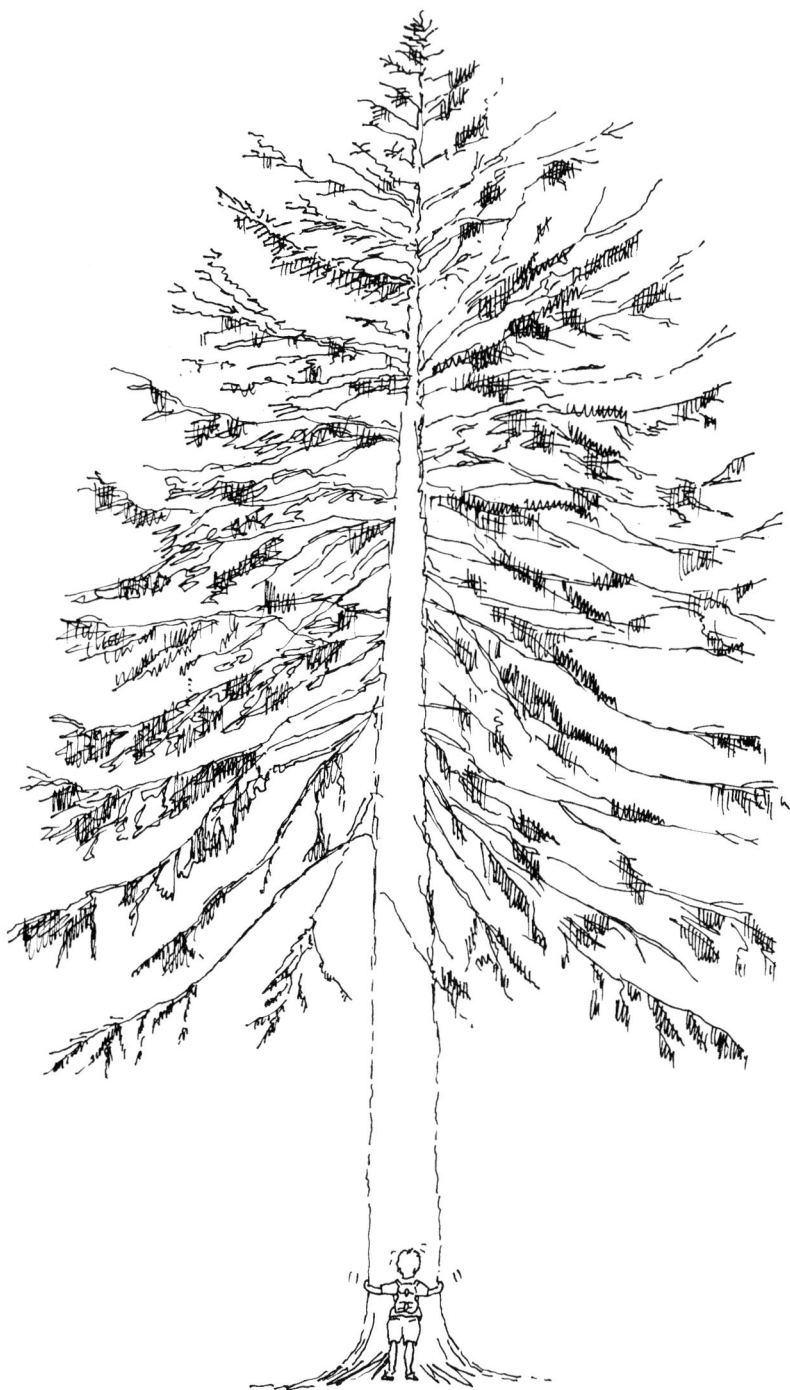

CHAPTER 10 - The Mightiest Conifer In Europe

The increasing distances between places I can stay means I'm cycling fewer miles each day than I'm capable of doing. This is really frustrating

My destination for today is the hostel at Inverary, which is only about six miles away due north on the other side of the loch, but twenty one miles by road. The bicycle chain is silent again so I must have done the right thing in waxing it. Although it's cloudy, disappointing after last night's calm and sunny evening, it's not raining and after about ten miles of beautiful cycling along the side of Loch Fyne, I reach the A83 and turn right. Almost immediately there's a sign to the Ardkinglas Woodland Garden which draws me off the main road and down a steeply wooded hill, which I realise with a sinking heart I shall have to trudge up again eventually.

Nevertheless, I have, by happy accident, discovered a treasure, and for two hours am in a state of awe-struck pleasure at the beauty of the trees and admiration for the management of this great estate. A leaflet says that the environmental conditions are perfect for woodland - the site is at sea level and relatively sheltered, and it enjoys a large annual rainfall with fertile free-draining sandy loam. Five of the trees here have been awarded Champion status. A Champion Tree is judged to be the tallest or broadest example in the British Isles by TROBI (Tree Register of the British Isles). Four of them were planted in the 1870s but the European Silver Fir was planted in 1750, making it over 250 years old and probably the oldest tree in the plantation. In 1905 it was 35 metres tall with a six metre girth, and an authority of the time called it "undeniably the mightiest conifer in Europe, if not the biggest bole of any living kind." It is a most extraordinary tree, very gnarled and full of character, and fortunately in the care of experts who love it.

FRESH POTATOE, LEEK + HADDOCK SOUP

If I had looked more carefully at my map, I would have seen that the side road I have come down rejoins the main road further on. Fortunately I discover this in time and avoid going back up the hill only to have had to come down it further along. Shortly, I come to a complex of tourist buildings - a Loch Fyne fish restaurant and snack bar, a garden centre and café, and a small delicatessen. I opt for a bowl of Cullen Skink soup for lunch and buy some smoked mackerel, oatcakes and apples for supper later on. Cullen Skink is the traditional Scottish dish of smoked haddock, potatoes and leeks, and is delicious. I resolve to find a recipe for it once I get home. The sun is growing less shy and mercifully it's becoming slightly warmer.

By the time I reach Inverary it's full-on hot and promises a beautiful evening. It is one of the most gracious Georgian towns in Britain with a tiny harbour and the loveliest of castles, which happened to be the favourite visiting place of Gavin Maxwell, the naturalist and author of *Ring of Bright Water,* when one of his friends lived there. I eat an ice-cream, appreciating the day I've had, feeling relaxed and competent!

At dead on five o'clock, the hostel opens, and I'm the first to register. I hasten to have my shower before the hordes arrive. I'm sharing a small room with two German sisters who examine my bike thoughtfully. I think they are admiring it, but they're really approving the Schwalbe tyres - you won't have any trouble with them, they assert confidently. Naturally! All the same, this increases my own confidence in them - naturally!

I spend a companionable evening in a sunny corner of the dining room chatting to others. There's Essex Man, who knows the Highlands intimately because he spends every single holiday trekking there; Lancashire Man who's travelling around Scotland with a rucksack and camera; an Australian couple who are on their way to join other members of their clan for a big family get-together in a castle owned by one of them; and an American family who generously allow everybody else to share their conversation. And the two German sisters and their husbands. It's a catholic gathering and the evening has a good feeling to it. The sun streams through the windows all evening making me very conscious of how important the sunshine is to my well-being. I am also aware of how much longer the daylight hours are up here, and increasingly conscious that my cycling has become a bit 'soft', ie, I am not doing many miles a day, and it's quite level.

The hostel warden informs me that there's a café in an old train carriage near Lochawe, so I have somewhere to aim for for mid-morning coffee. The ride due north from Inverary is splendid, with the majestic Ben Cruachan gradually exposing its oo-er factor as one crests a long incline running alongside Glen Aray. It's part of an impressive range of hills, some being Bens, others called Beinn or Sgorr, and I wonder what the difference is.

I stop for a few minutes to look at Kilchurn Castle which is perched on an island in the middle of Loch Awe itself. For a few blessed moments there's silence from the traffic. Then from across the water one can just about hear very faintly, the elusive notes of pipes coming and going on the breeze. It's piquantly pleasurable not to be able to hear them more clearly!

On reaching the A85 I could turn left or right, as I'm making for Fort William. Not today, of course, but that's where I'm heading for. Left is the long way round via Connel, the edge of Loch Linnhe and North Ballachulish. Right would be shorter, going over Rannoch Moor and through Glen Coe. What wonderful names and even more wonderful landscapes to cycle through. The loneliness of the moors and the grandeur of Glen Coe - just around the corner from here. I suppose I think of them as the centre of Scotland, the most dramatic places of my entire trip. The ones I've been longing to see. The places which were definitely on my itinerary, that were a most looked forward to part of the route. So I turn left! I guess I'm just chickening out because there are even fewer black dots along that road than the other.

Left it is, round the top of Loch Awe. And out of nowhere comes a twee two-carriage train, which reminds me to watch out for the café. And there it is - a totally stationary single carriage situated between the railway line and the shores of the Loch, with potted geraniums festooning a small garden area. The girl who runs it is giving a fresh coat of paint to various bits and bobs outside, so I sit in solitary splendour inside with a mug of tea. The interior is not quite so glamorous as the outside, but I have to indulge in nostalgia for the days when trains' interiors were made of polished timber and really did go chuff chuff!

I continue along the A85 which brings me to the Pass of Brander, reminding me once again of Lord of the Rings. Doesn't quite have the ring! of the the Gap of Gondor, but all the same, I'm surrounded on both sides by tall hillsides which cast the River Awe into almost permanent shade. The Pass is not as gloomy or sinister as I'd hoped/feared it might be, as the road itself is level and easy to ride.

I want to find a quiet picnic place to eat my lunch - Airds Bay fits the bill. It's shown as a cul de sac on my map, a little bay on the shores of Loch Etive. Apart from a few houses on its only road, and some industrial chimneys far away on the other side, it's an isolated little beach, and the perfect place to rest. On the ride today I have heard cuckoos and seen a dead deer and a dead heron, both extremely upsetting. I have been shocked at how much carnage there is on the roads; of squirrels, hedgehogs, rabbits, pheasants, even a robin and a finch, and crows without number. None of it caused by cyclists! My concentration on the road surface is such that I even see tiny little insects setting off to get to the other side, their journey seeming to them just as long as mine does to me, no doubt!

I arrive in Connel at about three, where I have booked a room in a B&B. The landlady, Margaret, is welcoming, saying her other guest is also a cyclist. I'm told that there's plenty of hot water for a bath - wonderful - and feeling refreshed I contemplate the bed for half an hour's siesta.....

Two and a half hours later - I wake up and promptly want to go back to sleep again, but I make myself get up and go out for an evening stroll in the sun to the local hotel, which Margaret tells me is the best place around for bar snacks. She says she would come with me, which I think is a really lovely offer, but she has been gardening and doesn't want the hassle of getting cleaned up. I can see from various certificates on the walls that she is a fitness instructor and a swimming teacher, and she does look extremely slim and agile for someone I would guess is roundabout my age. I also like her taste in books, which are absolutely everywhere. I recognise all the books I read growing up – H E Bates, Vicky Baum (whoever's heard of 'Marion Alive' or 'Grand Hotel' these days?), Neville Shute, etc. etc. Such familiar names.

She's right about the food - Thai fish cakes, garlic bread and a glass of wine are excellent. At the next table is a lone young man and we chat amiably as we eat, agreeing we should have had a bottle between us rather than two separate glasses. He's in need of more refreshment after his dinner and invites me for another drink at the bar, but I decline. The Chelsea Flower Show calls on TV and I want to watch it. Much as I would like to be there myself, it's always too crowded, and I've got used to being the only person in the universe.

Poring over my map, I am intrigued by the different names of the hills which I later find out are descriptive, eg ben and beinn mean hill; cnoc means knoll; maol indicates a bald-shaped top; rhu, rubha mean point, and squirr means pointed; sron means nose; and tom means rounded hillock. In long ago days when people only had oral knowledge to go by, with no maps or roads, latitude or longitude to pinpoint places, descriptions were necessary for social and wartime engagements.

"Let's meet at the western foot of the squirr sron" would have been more efficient than saying "Let's meet at the foot of the hill that's slightly to the left of that small hill which is second right to the big hill but not to be confused with the middling big hill with the trees on it, and there we can discuss the Chieftain's plans to make new paths through our fields for his own nefarious purposes"!

Margaret breakfasts with me, and we discover we have many things in common, among them the fact that both her brothers live not so far away from me, near London. Although she is English, she would now not want to live anywhere but Scotland. Her life revolves around music and the orchestras she plays in. Once again I have found somewhere I would like to stay for a while, but once again the unknown road beckons and, although I don't have a deadline to meet, I can't meander too much.

Having said that though, before reaching the hostel at Onich tonight, I do plan a slight detour to Ballachulish because a) I like the name and b) the map indicates a tourist attraction - Highland Mysteryworld - which I can't resist. It's a wonderful, panoramic ride along the side of Loch Linnhe, with the hills ahead of me. One of them is streaked with what looks like snow. Is it Ben Nevis? Yes, it is, and yes, it's snow. Just before lunch, I pass a road sign saying that one has now reached the Highlands, which is funny because I thought I already had. I find the Scottish counties as confusing as the French Departements.

Ballachulish is a very pretty village, with a rather cross Tourist Information Officer. When I enquire about the Highland Mysteryworld he says it's been shut for three years (my map is a 2003 edition), and that only last year the *Oban Times* had published a long article about it as if it were still an active concern, and as 93,000 visitors a year pass through Ballachulish he gets tired of having to explain that it is no longer open, and I can quite see why he gets cross. I'm cross myself as I'd hoped to learn a bit about Highland history and culture and the clans, as I am in the mood for such things today, but never mind....

A fleeting plan to detour further afield to Glencoe is abandoned - the thought of having to retrace my steps is too awful so it's a fairly early stop at Onich.

The hostel is situated in a small area of holiday caravans and chalets. The 12-bed female dormitory is uninhabited for tonight, apart from myself. I sit in a sunny spot under a tree and have a glass of wine and talk to a couple called Brian and Margaret who give me advice about tomorrow's road towards Fort William. It's a beautiful evening and when the sun goes down I have a bowl of soup in the bistro/bar and retire to the empty dormitory.

The plan for today, Day 32, is to stay in a B&B at Spean Bridge, going via Fort William. As if there were a choice! At this point, there's only one option.

The weather has deteriorated into rain and, again, a fresh northerly breeze. What's this about the prevailing wind? As I ride into Fort William my spirits lift on sighting Brian and Margaret. Last night I'd told them I was running out of my precious rehydrating powder and they have been looking out for me, kind souls, to lead me to a cycle shop where I stock up on more of the pink powder, which I have tried without success to buy in previous towns. It was beginning to worry me, as I really cannot drink the amount of pure water that one is supposed to, and from my experience of the first part of my trip, I know it is absolutely essential. I feel I've won the lottery as I leave the shop with my pink treasure!

Brian and Margaret remind me of a track called the Great Glen Way which starts at Fort William, and which vaguely caught my attention weeks ago at home when my eyes were glued to the map each day. It's a 'primrose path' running parallel to the River Lochy as an alternative to the A82 all the way to Inverness - a distance of roughly 64 miles. The Tourist Information Office doesn't seem to have any free leaflets on it, so I quickly scan a book giving complicated instructions on finding its beginning, and set off.

It's unbelievable! This is a much publicised, fairly new route which gives walkers and cyclists access to quiet forest roads and canal towpaths. It's a wonderful facility, but ridiculously complicated and frustrating to find the start. The pathway goes through a supermarket car park, wends its way over an ancient bridge hidden amongst a brand new suburban housing estate, then hides itself within an overgrown meadow, before emerging to join a lane running alongside a wire fence, finally to become a little woodland trail which actually, at last, is marked as the Great Glen Way. After a short while, the trail merges with a towpath along the Caledonian Canal.

Feeling triumphant at this victory I immediately cross, for some reason, to the other side of the canal and continue my way along the towpath for about a mile. But my all-singing-all-dancing mood of joie de vivre ends abruptly. My enhanced navigational skills employed so successfully a moment ago have obviously failed me at the very point of smug self-satisfaction a while ago. I am confronted by a level crossing with a stern notice forbidding unauthorised persons to cross the line - under any circumstances. Since a nearby signal box is strategically placed to notice everything happening in its vicinity, I reluctantly turn round and cycle the mile back to the lock gates, cross over and continue once again on the right path, having noticed with some chagrin another finger-pointing sign which I had failed to see before.

A lively crowd has gathered near to where one can cross the line legitimately, looking expectant. Here, at the foot of Neptune's Staircase, something is about to happen. A distant warning whistle sounds and then, instead of a city express roaring through, a steam train appears, the Jacobite it's called, the very one used as Hogwarts Express in the Harry Potter films, travelling from Fort William to Mallaig in a stately, measured progress. Train buffs and Harry Potter fans sitting inside stare out at us with as much interest as we stare in at them, but we have the best view of this lovely train as it passes slowly in a cloud of steam and well-mannered burps and snorts, with another distant whistle before turning the corner out of sight. Being an ardent Harry Potter fan, I'm delighted to see concrete evidence that Hogwarts exists!

Although Neptune's Staircase is marked on the map, it provides no indication of what it is. It turns out to be a staircase of nine lock gates within a very short distance – not *the* most spectacular series of locks in the canal system, but impressive nevertheless. There are tourists around looking interested, but there's no information to feed our curiosity - even the public lavatories are shut. It would be nice to know more. Visit Scotland doesn't seem very alert to the needs of curious, or even non-curious-just-need-a-lavatory, tourists.

It's a pleasant, but rather isolated and lonely ride along the towpath towards Gairlochy and the weather gradually deteriorates. A man sits on a bench by the turnoff to the road. We exchange a few words; he's walking to Inverness but knows that the next hostel on the route is too far away to reach this evening, so is contemplating his next move. He has very little food with him, he tells me, and we both know there's no shop for miles. He politely declines the apple and oat cakes which I offer him, then we go our separate ways.

I welcome the change of emphasis on food which this journey is imposing on me. Food is important in my life, and in the usual domestic setting much of my time is spent in shopping, cooking and eating. Without doubt I would prefer that it did not dominate my time so much, but I now relish the opportunity to treat it as a basic requirement. Small pleasures become more intense, reminding me of Indian sages who can spend an entire morning peeling and eating an orange. It would be nice to learn the art of savouring.

The five miles to Spean Bridge are like Cornwall again - steep hills and beautiful landscape, with Ben Nevis somewhere over to my right, but the wind is getting up and the rain is coming down and I'm not in the mood to have a look at a rather magnificent monument at the junction of the A82. I do, however, feel a sudden yen to re-read John Buchan's 'Thirty Nine Steps' again. Were some of the scenes set near here, I wonder?

On arrival at the B&B I am shown to my room which feels like a chilly cell. An electric heater is vaguely pointed out at the end of the tour of my room, which I attempt to turn on without success. There's a dial with some tiny little levers which I play with but again nothing happens. I find a switch deeply embedded in a little niche which one would need a talon to operate so I reckon that can't be significant. I give in and consult my host, who tut tuts at the state of the little levers which apparently have something to do with the timer, and I can feel the atmosphere becoming even chillier. With a deft movement the switch which I thought was inaccessible, is turned on and heat slowly drifts into the room. I set out to explore what is my space for the next 16 hours or so, and acquaint myself with the bed, which is the only thing to sit on, the TV which produces a fascinating picture of snow, the window through which one can only see sky, and the chest of drawers which can be opened as long as nobody stands in front of it. Inside one of the drawers is a magazine, and after I've had a shower, eaten my supper, written up my notes, checked on tomorrow's route, done my washing, filed my nails, and spring-cleaned my panniers, I still have 14 hours left to fill before I can escape to breakfast, so I read it.

It tells of things I did not know about the Celtic civilisation. That it lasted 2,000 years and eventually disintegrated because of its argumentative nature. Among the Greek and Roman descriptions of the Celts are "quarrelsome", "boastful", "insolent", and "proud". These adjectives, though, are a mite simplistic. At its height, it was a dazzling civilisation, its boundaries reaching from the Atlantic through most of Spain and Central Europe to Eastern Turkey. Although a picture of a barbaric and warmongering people has prevailed due to the influence of classical history, the Celts were also artists of sensitivity and ingenuity, highly skilled smiths, builders and miners, and merchants who traded successfully in the international arena.

Because it was such an extensive civilisation, it naturally had no recognisable set of distinctive characteristics which were common to all. They were, rather, groups of societies whose customs differed from each other. However, two characteristics common to most of these unhomogenised groups comprise a love, and a sophisticated expression through art, of nature in all its forms; and a belief in an afterlife and the fluid boundaries between this world and the Otherworld, with journeys able to be undertaken to and from both sides at special times of the year. Because of their understanding of the fluidity of the cosmos, they could accept the ideas of transformation between humans and animals, and also of magic.

Two expanding cultures hastened the demise of the Celtic civilisation - the Germanic tribes to the north, and the Romans to the south - and by 500 AD it was in retreat, with the exception of Ireland, which hung on long enough to have another golden age.

Although it is a spent force, there are still Celtic influences in our modern lives today, and they may have survived because of the lack of rigidity, the acceptance of change and flexibility that underlay the very foundation of the Celtic civilisation.

Maybe it's making a come-back, as all place names in Scotland now are written in Gaelic as well as English.

The same magazine also tells me that the national strategy for tourism in Scotland promotes three niche markets: golfing holidays, cultural tourism and genealogy. The latter is centred on the Isle of Harris at the Genealogy Centre. There are 30,000 families covering all the Western Isles which are featured there. As for golf, Scotland is where it all started, and I have passed many courses in recent days. But I am not quite sure what 'cultural tourism' means, unless it's the taped bagpipes in the Fort William Tourist Office!

The closer I get to John O'Groats the more I find myself thinking about how I shall feel when the trip is over. At the moment I'm enjoying this life style. Exercise, fresh air, always on the move, meeting new people, no responsibilities, beautiful scenery, and easy cycling. Even though the weather leaves a bit to be desired I'm not at all sure I want to reach journey's end. Will this trip whet my appetite for more? Or will I feel fatly (and flatly) contented to sit by the fireside and reminisce for the rest of my life? Only time will tell.

CHAPTER 11 - Does It Always Rain In Scotland?

After breakfast comes escape from my prison and I set out with relief for Fort Augustus. All the 'Fort' names along the way remind me of cowboy and Indian films but the settlers of the American West would have used all these names from back home in Britain in the first place, presumably, so the process of word association is the wrong way round.

Having to retrace my steps back to Gairlochy to rejoin the Great Glen Way I pass the monument I spotted yesterday, but this time feel more inclined to stop and inspect it. I'm very glad I do, because it is a touching memorial to the Commando Unit created by Winston Churchill as an elite corps of highly trained soldiers (afterwards known as the SAS), who were actually trained near here. This is the weather to appreciate how hard it must have been - and this is summer! - but the ruggedness of the three soldiers shown dressed in their full fighting kit reflects the toughness of the landscape that they gaze out upon for as long as these hills remain.

As I stare up at the statue I am joined by an elderly gentleman who tells me he worked as an engineer for the Commandos, and he's making his annual pilgrimage to the area to stay with the very same couple who had looked after him in their B&B when he was undergoing training as a young man. I comment that they must be quite an age themselves now to be running such a business but he says they are not in business anymore - he's an honoured guest each year. It's a truism to say that people's lives are still affected by events which took place 60-odd years ago but when you hear of a particular detail it does make one especially thoughtful. He also tells me that he doesn't suffer from rheumatism at all because he rubs dog oil into the backs of his knees whenever he feels it coming on. He gets his dog oil from someone in Lancaster. I think the dog oil is oil used on greyhounds and store the information away with the lumps of root ginger to research further once I'm home. It has been a privilege to talk to him.

The Great Glen Way continues as a forest trail from Gairlochy. By this time, the trees and I are dripping with a relentless drizzle. After about nine miles, the forest and the trail suddenly end and I find myself on a very busy road which I have to guess is the A82 joining us from the other side of Loch Lochy but I can't be sure as my glasses are wet, my tissues are too disintegrated to dry them, the map's a sodden pulp, my hair is hanging over my eyes like rats' tails, and I feel hungry. I don't know where I am and there's no dry spot to sit down anywhere, so I eat my damp sandwich standing up under a tree, trying to think. I am completely disorientated and am not sure whether to turn right or left along this horrid traffic infested road, but I decide that probably left is right so plod on. I shortly come to a general stores but what I really need is a café in which to sit down and have a hot cup of tea, so I just buy a chocolate bar to have an excuse to be in a dry place for a few minutes. I leave, having completely forgotten to ask where I am!

A few miles further on I catch a glimpse of a hotel and a small Heritage Centre, which are situated at the junction with the A87, just before reaching Invergarry. Knowing that I'll be tempted to get too comfortable in the hotel, I opt for the museum, which is tiny. All I want is to sit down for a few minutes in the dry, but I pay my pound to get inside the door and then have to appear interested while the history of Glengarry and its various characters is explained to me personally, while I'm standing wet as a mermaid. When I rather feebly say to the well-informed historian that, although I would like to look and learn in more detail another time, I think I need to do something about possible pneumonia, he suggests I go to the hotel to dry off. But what's the point if I'm only going to get wet again? I just want to sit down and have someone hand me a hot mug of tea.

Continuing on my travels I make the mistake of turning right outside the museum, instead of left towards Invergarry. All these Garrys and Invers have confused me, but I suspect something is wrong after about three miles. I check with a couple who are standing by their car, also conferring with their map, and realise I'm on the way to the Kyle of Lochalsh and the Isle of Skye instead of Fort Augustus and John O'Groats. Never mind, the rain is beginning to ease a bit and the gloom is lifting. By the time I get to the Bridge of Oich and rejoin the Great Glen Way running alongside the Caledonian Canal, the sun breaks through and I'm beginning to dry off. Ahead of me, along this quiet towpath, strides a figure which turns out to be the man I left sitting, foodless, on the bench yesterday. We greet each other as old friends and travel a couple of miles together. I ask how he had fared the previous night. He, John, says he found an excellent place to bivouac, and feasted on four Ryvita biscuits spread with olive oil and salt, and as it had been a Friday night treated himself to a sachet of pepper as well! Plus half a Mars bar. I love this! I love the way one's appreciation of the simple things is heightened when the usual 'plenty' is not so plentiful for a while. We have a most interesting philosophical conversation on Life in General and All That. He tells me, too, that the hostel I am bound for, and into which I'm booked for the night, is full for the Bank Holiday weekend - he tried too late to make a reservation, but he might try it again, in person, all the same.

There is a Tourist Information shop at Fort Augustus, where I buy, not *The Thirty Nine Steps,* which unsurprisingly they don't stock, but *Polly - The True Story Behind Whisky Galore* by R Hutchinson. I'm not sure why, but as my panniers don't feel as heavy as they did before, I'm prepared to carry the extra weight of a book.

When I check in at the hostel the warden tells me that he could have let out the beds four times over. I feel sorry for John as it looks as though it will be another night bivouac-ing, but at seven o'clock he appears in the kitchen. We are both puzzled because we hear the warden turn away five other hikers, and it turns out that both of us have a spare bunk in our rooms! Added to that, we can only count seventeen other occupants in the hostel when the literature says it can take thirty three people. What's going on, we wonder, though without reaching any conclusion at all.

It is turning into a beautiful evening, and we join a couple who are sitting outside drinking their wine in the evening sunshine, listening to a guitar being softly strummed inside. It's sociable company, and a far cry from yesterday.

CHAPTER 12 - Myths And Monsters

Eleven of the hostellers are American: ten mixed - teenagers I would guess - with one male teacher. At breakfast, I remark to him that they must be quite a responsibility, and he nods, but "so far, so good," he says with a serene smile. The man's a saint! He's used to accompanying pupils to Scotland as the school they belong to is one which specialises in environmental subjects. This particular group is cycling the Great Glen Way all the way to Inverness and I have to admit that some of it has been too much - too hilly and rough for both my bike and me - but they have managed it on their mountain bikes. Last night I observed the quiet way he let them get on with cooking their supper. They were very vocal and consultative with each other, while he just allowed them to sort things out for themselves, with just a tweak of comment here and there. They are not at all curious about me and display a lack of curiosity I've noticed before among North American students: when he tells them, "This lady is cycling all the way from Land's End to John O'Groats," one or two politely comment "That's cool!".

I don't expect or want to be held up as an intrepid voyager but I have come to expect the usual questions of how long will it take, how many miles a day, and, of course, why and what for?

I bid good-bye to John and the convivial couple of last evening and depart at 8.50 am. John is off to the next hostel along the way, giving himself an easy walk to Invermoriston as a break. It's such a lovely morning that I only cycle three and a quarter miles before I make my first pit stop on a seat in the sun overlooking Loch Ness. Intuition tells me to make the most of the fine weather and my second stop is at 10.40. I eat some nuts and discover wild raspberries growing nearby – too early in the season to eat, unfortunately - and watch and listen to the numerous finches fluttering around. It's like sitting in an aviary. Loch Ness looks like glass and I feel meditative in the hot sun with only the sound of the birds to break the silence.

I'm beginning to feel the fitness effects of cycling every day and am pleased to see that my shadow seems less bulky than usual. Perhaps that's because the sun is climbing higher each day? When I pass a pool I'm so tempted to have a dip. It looks sparkling clean and cold. It is too small to swim in, but looks deep enough for complete coverage. I contemplate the sheer heaven of wild dipping, the sheer hell of icy agony, the difficulty of climbing down into it, and reluctantly decide against the idea.

Progress is slow this morning. After two and three quarter hours I've travelled nine and a quarter miles, but I'm in no hurry. I've booked in at a hostel at Drumnadrochit and have plenty of time. I pass Urqhuart Castle and feel I should visit at least one Scottish castle sometime, but looking at the steepness of the slope down to it I decide that this is not the one. Later on, Will tells me we have already visited it, many years ago, but I can't remember.

It's Sunday today and this is a really easy day's ride. I reach Drumnadrochit in the early afternoon, and pass a junior gymkhana taking place at the foot of a rather steep hill. The boys and girls look very young, but extremely competent on their ponies. Horse riding is yet another thing I cannot do, and I think they are very brave youngsters. I don't, however, add it to my list of things to do. It can wait until I've done everything else!

The local Tourist Office has masses of information on Loch Ness and Nessie of course, and I soon find myself at the Loch Ness exhibition. It's fascinating to learn that Scotland started off below the equator and spent five hundred million years moving to its present position at the pace of a growing finger nail. The question one cannot ask the disembodied voice conveying all the information was - does this include the rest of Britain too? But it is the mystery of the Loch Ness Monster which is obviously given the most attention. All the photographs of 'sightings' of Nessie have been explained in one way or another: by swimming deer (unusual but not unknown); swooping seagulls; the wash from boats; or hoaxes. Although it is the largest lake in Britain, holding more water than England and Wales together, and with enough volume to cover the world three times over, it still would not provide enough food to feed a Nessie. However, the sophisticatedly equipped modern boats are still out there, scanning the depths for yet more information from the all but impenetrable depths.

The weather has deteriorated again, with ominous looking clouds gathering overhead. I book into the hostel, but its hippy atmosphere makes me feel uncomfortable and after quickly sorting my stuff out, I cycle a short distance to the nearby café/bar which advertises all-day food. But there's no food at all at the moment, as the chef is late. I wait for about an hour, then everybody who has ordered food receives a bowl of soup. The chef has still not come, we are told, and this is the best thing the remaining staff can come up with. In the meantime, the heavens have opened, and I settle down in a comfy, shabby sofa opposite a young couple, for what is obviously going to be a long evening. There's a pool table in the centre of the room, and the atmosphere is one of cheerful sociability as the cloudburst continues. We are all temporarily trapped - maybe the chef is prophetic. The young couple, Connor and Angela, are camping on the gymkhana hillside I passed earlier and are wondering - remarkably unperturbed - how their tent and belongings are faring. It *is* a rather steep hillside, and they are imagining water pouring through their tent and washing everthing down the hill. Although there's nothing on earth they can do about it at the moment, I still think they show admirable sang froid. Being Irish, Connor keeps me entertained by his talk, which pours forth like the rain. I am in full agreement with his complaint about motorcyclists, whose noise, speed and numbers are so tormenting to us cyclists, particularly on Sundays, when dozens of them zoom up and down the roads in large groups at breakneck speed.

During a break in the downpour, I take my leave of my two temporary companions and this friendly, busy, inefficient little café and make a dash for the hostel. The staff saw my towel hanging out to dry earlier and have brought it in for me - but only after it had already got sodden. They hand this dripping object over to me, proudly, as if to say: "Weren't we thoughtful?"! I find it difficult to say "thank you" with sincere gratitude, as it was no drier than if they had left it out.

CHAPTER 13 - Inside The Castle Walls

I discovered last night that perhaps I'm not quite the lemon I thought I was on my first night in St Just when I asked if it was the hostel's policy to have mixed dormitories. Two of the six incumbents in my room last night were male. So my query, all those months ago, had not been so inappropriate after all! But everyone was amazingly discreet.

Drumnadrochit is where I leave the Great Glen Way and strike north for my next stop, which is at Dingwall where I have booked a room in a B&B. So I exit the town by the A833, having been warned that this road is a 'big hill'. When I see the sign indicating a 15% gradient I immediately dismount, unlike a couple who pass me on a tandem. We call out cheery greetings and I watch them wobble their way up and round a corner.

The warnings are justified. Almost six miles of climbing before the road starts to level out, but once on the top the view is wonderful. Quite bleak, with the weather to match, although it is dry - for the moment. The next eight or nine miles to Beauly are quiet, undulating roads, and a pleasure to be on.

I stop off at the Beauly Scottish Centre for a glass of raspberry juice and an enormous scone, cream and jam. Judging by the quality and quantity of Scottish goodies for sale, this must be a very popular destination for tourists, although today it's rather empty. On my way out of the little town I notice that the Tourist Office is shut - this is a Bank Holiday Monday.

It's a flat road through the Muir of Ord – more shades of Tolkein - but the semi-industrial, suburban nature of its environs doesn't live up to the promise of the name. Soon after, I am caught up by a fellow cyclist who is also on his way to John O'Groats. Although he slows down to match my meandering progress, being accompanied does act as a catalyst to put a spurt on, and we reach Dingwall soon after 1 pm. It's far too early to stop as planned and, after studying the map, I decide to go on to Evanton. Fellow Cyclist is staying at Carbisdale Castle hostel which is too far away for me to get to today, besides which, examining the map yesterday, I noticed it's on the wrong side of the Kyle of Sutherland, and that I would have to back track to Ardgay to rejoin the A836 on the following day. He assures me there is now a footbridge over the railway station at Culrain, close to the castle, to meet up with the A836 which eliminates the need to backtrack. All the same, I feel it's still too far.

After a short chat, in which I discover that he stayed last night at the same hostel as John at Invermoriston, and spent the evening with him, we part company - he to follow the CTC route through the minor roads and me to continue on the main roads to Evanton. In next to no time I have reached and gone beyond it. The next possible stop where I might find accommodation looks to be Alness, a town slightly to the west of where I am heading. But from a distance, it looks ominously industrial and does not appeal at all. A snap decision and I opt for the B9176 which wends its way northwards with very very few signs of habitation marked on the map. Now this is something I have vowed not to do again, particularly on a Bank Holiday weekend - to launch myself off into the unknown - and it's getting on for three o'clock. What on earth am I doing? I seem unable to stop cycling today. It's turned into a fine afternoon and I give myself a break. The scone has done me very well so far, but I'm flagging now and feeling slightly stressed with nowhere to stay, which is entirely my own fault as I just can't stop moving. The road is quiet and while I sit on a sunny grass bank, munching a power bar, I idly ponder on the possibility of getting to the Castle tonight, after all. I make a leisurely fumble for my mobile and am surprised to find the signal is strong here. The hostel brochure happens to be easily to hand and I cast my eye sluggishly down the list of phone numbers. My fingers slowly press the buttons and a voice immediately answers. Not expecting anything to be easy on a Bank Holiday Monday I'm astonished to hear that they do actually have a bed free for tonight. What's more, they don't shut the doors until 10.30 pm. Yes! I am suddenly far from sluggish at the thought that tonight I am sleeping in a castle, have ample time to get there, and it's a beautiful afternoon!

How quickly one's mood can change. I feel galvanised with happiness and energy. It's *so* comforting to know there's a bed for me and all I have to do is get to it! I rather guiltily phone the B&B at Dingwall to cancel tonight, feeling bad about doing so, but this is the problem with booking ahead.

This road is fairly flat, although it's at quite a high altitude, and with some foreboding I see ahead of me what could be the low pressure weather front which is vying with the high pressure front from the south, which Will tells me is the cause of the unsettled conditions I have not been enjoying. Behind me, the sun - warmth, clear skies, and pleasantness. In front - cold, clammy mist and claustrophobic visibility. It must be mists like this which inspired the story of Brigadoon, the village which appears just once every hundred years. What shall I find on the other side? Will it still be the 21st century?

It's a strange feeling, cyling into the white swirling mist. It is quiet, with only the occasional muffled sound of a bird calling. Visibility is very limited and the world has suddenly shrunk. It's quite chilly but not clammy. The occasional car passes going the other way, so at least they have cars on the other side! After about fifteen minutes of this eerie experience, the light brightens, and I feel the welcome warmth of the sun once again. In addition, there is a magnificent view over the Dornoch Firth. The road surface of the A836, which I now join, is another pleasure. It is undoubtedly the best I've cycled on in Scotland yet, and I speed down this long, smooth, dead straight gradient like greased lightning. Glancing at the odometer I see that for a few seconds

I'm travelling at 29 mph, which I think is probably the fastest I've ever gone. I reluctantly use my brakes, wishing I was courageous enough to just let go completely.

At Ardgay I pass the turn off to Bonar Bridge, and after buying myself a salad supper in a corner shop, I start the final lap to the Castle along minor, scenic roads to Culrain.

Arriving at the Castle is a wonderful moment! It's a splendid building, but quite new as castles go - less than a century old, but full of character and space. It was built between 1906 and 1917 for the Dowager Duchess of Sutherland and described, I later discover, by *The Rough Guide to Scotland* as 'one of the most opulent youth hostels in the world'. One long gallery only has a table-tennis table in it. Another, just statues and pictures, with people wandering around looking quite dazed. The first person I bump into is Fellow Cyclist, who introduces me to the tandem duo who had passed me this morning, and who are also on their way to JOG. Wendy and Dan had managed to cycle *almost* to the top of the horrendous hill, but hadn't *quite* made it. They brought welcome news with them, having camped the previous evening on a hillside just outside Drumnadrochit, their tenting neighbours being - Angela and Connor. Apparently, all had been well when they returned to their tent - nothing had been washed away which strikes me as little short of a miracle.

Another face I recognise is that of Lancastrian Man from Inverary hostel. Carbisdale Castle is very popular with all hostellers and people take a bit of trouble getting here. He has been staying several nights on a photographic mission, and leaves for home in the morning. He confirms that there is a bridge crossing to the main road at the bottom of the castle drive and will himself be travelling on the train from the little Culrain station. He tells me it's taken him three days to discover that there's a games room, apart from the table tennis gallery, so there's a lot to explore, but very little time for me to do it in. Must return! It's a busy evening as I have to cancel tomorrow's booking at Bonar Bridge, have a long phone conversation with Will catching up on family news, clothes-drying from yesterday to organise, and exchanging travellers' titbits with all these people I've met. Not to mention having supper.

My odometer reads 55 miles - this is only the second time I've hit the fifties, and my best so far. This is also the day that I pass the 1,000 mile mark. Perhaps, subconsciously, that's why I just kept going.

I notice there's no sunset - the clouds are gathering.

CHAPTER 14 - A Touch Of Zen

I sleep in a large room occupied by three others, one of whom is Wendy. We chat as we drift off to sleep - mainly about highway safety for cyclists. She knows the subject well, and maintains that cyclists have to claim their share of the road. My tactic is to stick out slightly further than absolutely necessary until I hear or sense the motorist behind me slow down, when I will then move nearer to the inside edge to allow him to pass. I feel this is safer than permanently hugging the inner edge to allow motorists to shoot past without pausing for thought. But, as with most things, each situation is unique. Naturally, my own safety is of paramount importance to me - and indirectly also to the motorist. If I make it easier for him not to knock me down, he benefits too. The motorist should remember that for every cyclist on the road, there is one less car creating jams holding *him* up.

I wake to the gentle sound of rain. Besides my ubiquitous oat biscuits, cheese and apples, I make use of the anybody-can-have-it shelf and find sliced white bread and a big bucket of bright yellow margarine. They are more a chemical pretence at food, I feel, than the real stuff, but nevertheless breakfast and lunch of a sort are provided for, and I mustn't look a gift horse in the mouth I tell myself. Although in this instance the gift horse is actually going into the mouth. The reason I am often without much food is that I don't like going out of my way to find it. If a shop is there when I stop, then I'll stock up, but as much of my normal life is spent on food-related activities, it's a welcome break for me not to have to think about it much now. So, I make do with what's around.

By the time I've organised myself to leave, so has everybody else. Wendy and Dan are detouring to Cape Wrath, Fellow Cyclist has been given three weeks by his wife to do the End-to-End, so he's already departed to meet his deadline, and Lancastrian Man has caught an early train. I have said good-bye to all these people who've suddenly come into my life as new, if temporary friends, without even knowing some of their names.

People travelling like this seem to have an unconscious recognition of a temporary soulmate, and you can often find yourself having very intimate conversations, probably because you both know that you won't meet again, and the time spent on the road is so separate from home life. It is ironic, but somehow quite right, that I was unable to swap phone numbers with the one person I met that I would have liked to get in touch with again.

With everyone else gone, when I reach the bottom of the castle drive and cannot find the famous footbridge, there's nobody left to ask for more specific directions. Rather than dithering around in the increasing rain I make a quick decision to retrace - after all - yesterday's road to join the A836 at Ardgay, and thence to Bonar Bridge, where

I'm supposed to be staying tonight. That will only be about six miles away. Yesterday, I cycled almost three times as far as I had planned. It's irritating to have to backtrack, and I wish I'd taken more notice of yesterday's talk about the whereabouts of this famous connecting bridge.

I have also noticed that my odometer seems to be malfunctioning. I recall that, after recording the day's mileage in my notebook yesterday evening, I dropped it on to the floor, but thought no more about it. It normally records each day's mileage, which I bring back to zero at the beginning of each day, but goes on recording the total trip mileage in a hidden part of its mechanism, which I call up when I want to. On checking the other functions, I'm puzzled why they are working but not the daily mileage one. I have to be thankful that *something's* working, even though I now have no means of knowing how far I've cycled from A to B. Every evening now, I shall have to work out the day's mileage by deducting the previous day's overall figure from today's overall figure. It's a bore, but not a tragedy. But it's only 9 am and that's two setbacks already today!

It's a saturating ride to Lairg but I like the look of a sign saying The Nip Inn and stay drinking a pot of tea for about an hour. I have to spread my things around to dry them off but nobody seems to mind. There are two young girls, smoking and playing pool who appear to have the care of a baby in a pram. I watch them, as they squander their youth, health and beauty on these rather aimless activities, feeling like a disapproving school ma'am, and am very glad when the woman behind the bar tells them not to smoke - not for the baby's sake I understand, but because it's against the pub rules to smoke while playing pool!

A man offers me his newspaper to read but I decline, and instead we chat about this and that. He comes from a long line of fishermen, but although he has sons, the line will end with him. I think it's very sad. There are no more fish for them to catch, he

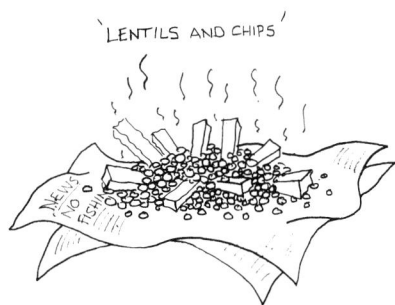
'LENTILS AND CHIPS'

says. What cod there is has apparently migrated to the colder waters of Iceland. I ask him what, in his view, is the reason for the declining fishing industry and he says it's down to the Spanish, the Japanese and global warming. I remember a conversation I had a few years ago with the wife of a Cornish fisherman, who had commented angrily to me that it was all the new Common Market inspectors interfering with Cornish fishing traditions that had ruined the industry. I would imagine that the people with a vested interest and with generations of experience in managing their resources would perhaps be the best people to be entrusted to continue with it. But politicians and bureaucrats like to feel they are relevant, so have to interfere to justify their existence. Fish stocks are now in crisis. We shall all have to eat lentils, which is good news for the fish.

As I cycle out of Lairg I am aware that, for the first time, I cannot see any pylons nor any sign of human habitation. Just an unfenced road ahead of me, along which there is only intermittent traffic. The hills are covered with brown heather, gently rolling on into the far distance, with nothing to spoil the view. It is lovely, lovely, lovely! Admittedly, there are a few of the usual straight-sided, dark green blobs indicating man-made forests, but they are small blobs and not too obvious. It is very quiet, without a background hum of traffic, just the occasional car or lorry. Nevertheless, without my little computer working properly, I don't know how far I've cycled. I don't like that, as it's a long empty road up to Altnaharra where I'm staying tonight, and in these particular conditions I would like to know how far I've gone so that I can orientate myself on the map. As it is, I keep an eye on my watch and how fast I'm going, and try to work out in my head how far, roughly speaking, I have travelled. That will have to do from now on, unless I find a brilliant computer mechanic somewhere.

After about an hour, the rain eases and I stop and, standing beside a cattle grid where I can prop up the bike, I eat my exciting sandwich. I feel unaccountably content as I stand there munching on damp cotton-wool bread. I attempt to analyse this unexpected feeling. Is it because the few drivers who do pass invariably toot and wave at me companionably? Is it because it has temporarily stopped raining? Or because I have nearly completed the trip? My conclusions at the end of this short self-psychoanalytical session is that it's because this particular scenery makes me feel free. At last I have actually reached a part of the country which is, itself, free - from pollution, noise, people, stress, over-stimulation, spin, ugliness, advertising. And I feel safe. I don't feel isolated, lonely or bored, or even hungry! I don't long for a drink, a film, a book, a companion, or a newspaper. For a little while, I feel I am in what I imagine to be a zen mode of being.

All the same, I don't linger long as it starts to rain again and now I'm cycling through the forests I have a chance to look at these unattractive green blobs close up. And I confess to being totally in thrall to their immensity and their variety. Larches, spruces, cedars, firs, pines, cypresses, standing upright like soldiers dressed in their full regimental uniforms. They are truly magnificent. I suppose the trees in the centre of the forest, where little light penetrates, will be all trunk and no trappings, so to speak. Some of the trees on the edge are quite small and their new growth sticks up like rude fingers which, in my present mood, makes me giggle hysterically. But I am now seriously cold and fed up. Zen moments by their very nature seem not to last very long.

Just before I lie down and die, the Crask Inn hoves into view. Although it's marked on my map, I didn't dare believe it would be an operational place of shelter and refreshment, but there it is, with six other bikes parked outside. Inside are six equally sopping cyclists, four of whom soon leave. Although my hot chocolate gives me much needed solace, and the other two cyclists are friendly, I feel I can't stay in my wet clothes for longer than absolutely necessary. The landlord wants to show me his puppies, though, which are utterly gorgeous, and by the time I take my leave the sun is feebly fighting its way through the clouds.

The next nine miles or so to Altnaharra are simply magical. Loch Naver is a glinting dagger of still water, and its juxtaposition with the background hills behind is so exquisitely beautiful it brings tears to my eyes. Altnaharra itself comprises the B&B, about 17 other souls and a smart hotel. I am advised that bad feeling between the management of the hotel and the locals, who comprised most of the staff, means that now the hotel has none! The proprietors of the B&B, Mandy and Lindsay, moved up here from Oxfordshire last year. They have never looked back, quickly finding a niche for themselves in this tiny hamlet and Lindsay is shortly to become the official weatherman of Altnaharra Weather Station. Dinner, starting with a second-to-none French onion soup, is cooked by Mandy, around whose table are also a Glaswegian gentleman and the Dutch couple from the Crask Inn - whose names, I learn, are Ine and Frits. They are cycling their way to John O'Groats as part of the North Sea Cycle Route which they are doing, piecemeal - a trip of around 6,000 kilometres. After dinner, through the large picture window in the living room with its spectacular unspoilt view of the loch and hills beyond, we watch the evening gathering of a herd of wild deer. Sutherland has 30,000 of them. Each year, just before the shooting season starts, they disappear. Nobody knows where to, they just vanish - into secret places only the deer know about. It's a nice thing to hear anyway...!

I have already forgotten the wet and miserable ride of this morning!

CHAPTER 15 - Sheep At Bedtime

After an excellent and sociable breakfast, I say goodbye to yet another place I don't really want to leave. From Altnaharra I have a choice of two roads - one, the most hilly and therefore most scenic, goes due north to Tongue; the other is flatter and more or less follows the River Naver to Bettyhill via Syre. I opt for the easier ride as I am told it is still beautiful, which turns out to be true.

The sky, as usual, is gloomy and overcast and, as usual there's a stiff breeze which I swear is from the north. But in the distance is a thin blueish-turquoise line which indicates the direction of the sea. I take numerous photos of boulders and rocks which are covered with the most subtly coloured lichens and mosses, and although I know I'll be disappointed at the results, cannot resist taking views of the Loch as well.

Passing through a tiny village, barking alerts me to a dog's far off presence. I have plenty of time to get out the dazer, check it's working and to resolve that if the dog dares to take so much as one step towards me, it'll get a dose of high frequency discomfort. He takes more than one step - he bounds towards me with a fiercesome snarl, which makes me wobble. Instead of confidently pointing the dazer at him directly, I wave it vaguely from side to side which has no effect whatsoever. By this time I've stopped cycling altogether and thankfully a woman appears at the front door. But she's no help at all. I shout at her to control her dog and she says, unabashedly untruthfully, that "Aim doin' ma best", while doing absolutely nothing. I tell her she should manage her beast properly and she says: "Ye should joost cycle faister!" She has a point, I suppose! I'm shaking like an aspen leaf as I start off again, with the dog still growling menacingly. But he hasn't actually bitten me, or torn the clothes off me!

It's only a large village, but Bettyhill seems a hive of activity after the loneliness of the last few miles and I stop at a café for a drink. Ine is also in the café, checking out the book shelf; she and Frits are picnicing in a sheltered spot nearby, so we chat again. It's nice to bump into people who have become familiar, but who are completely separated from my regular life. The last few days have felt cocooned in a world consisting of a handful of people, most of whom are focused on John O'Groats. Ine and Frits continue on their way and I sit for a while and enjoy the sunshine and sea air. At the risk of repeating myself, it is simply quite breathtaking.

There's a long incline out of Bettyhill and while I'm footslogging my way upwards I glance behind me and notice a figure slowly but surely gaining on me on wheels. It's difficult to determine whether it's male or female from a distance, but eventually I hear a German female voice greet me. I turn round and there beside me is a smiling, bronzed and gorgeous young woman. I immediately secretly name her Brunnhilde.

We stop at the top where there's a convenient picnic table, and study the landscape. It's rough and rugged, bleak and inhospitable, and easy to imagine the warmongering Celts ranging over these hills looking for trouble. But nowadays you can turn a corner and find a phone box and a bus stop.

Brunnhilde is like me, and there aren't many of us I realise, a woman travelling on her own and, like Frits and Ine, also cycling part of the North Sea Route. She was not happy during her first week or so of cycling along the east coast of England, camping most of the time in caravan parks. She found no-one to speak to and was lonely and did not find the countryside particularly attractive. Now, however, in Scotland she has found what she is looking for, and even the indifferent weather she feels is fitting to the landscape! She had stayed at Carbisdale Castle too and also like me had failed to find the footbridge across the Culrain railway line!

We say goodbye - she's eating her lunch while enjoying the view. Occasionally I glance behind me but for quite a while there's absolutely no sign of her. But then I see her, and again, slowly but surely she overtakes me with a friendly wave. She cycles on ahead not seeming to make any effort, graceful and stately, but making good ground all the same, and eventually she disappears from view round a hill, then reappears again in the far distance, until she disappears for good. Cycling along these undulating roads, around the brows of the hills, in the sunshine, is deeply pleasurable.

Arriving at the outskirt of Melvich I see Brunnhilde has stopped and waited for me to catch up. Her plan, on seeing the sand dunes on the beach, is to camp wild tonight. It saves money, and she has her own little cooking stove and everything she needs. I book into my farm B&B, right at the other end of Melvich, where the resident farm dog snaps and worries at my shorts. I think he thinks I'm a sheep and wants to herd me into a field with the other sheep. I debate whether to join Brunnhilde for an evening's sociability, but don't have the energy to get to the other end of town. Instead, I take myself off to a nearby pub and have some sweet and tender Orkney herrings for supper.

I retire early but before I go to sleep I'm alerted by a strange noise outside the window. It's an eerie noise and I peer out to investigate. In a nearby field, leaning against the fence is a sheep with her adolescent lamb hovering uncertainly close by. She is immobile, with her head held at an awkward angle and making strange noises. A van comes into the yard and out gets a young woman, who goes inside. After a moment or two she comes out, gets into the van and leaves, but neither she nor the driver seem to have noticed that something might be wrong with the animal. I'm not a country person, but by this time, the sheep has gradually slipped down and is lying on her side, and obviously something's seriously amiss. I guess I just have to tell someone. I get dressed again and go down to the kitchen, to find the farmer warming a very large baby's bottle on the stove. I tell him I have no wish to interfere (oh, dear, did I really say that?), but am sure one of his sheep is in deep distress. He points to the saucepan. He's warming up the medicine just delivered by the vet! He's not sure what's wrong, but it could be brain damage he tells me.

I go back to bed, pondering how sheep can have brain damage when they don't have any.

USEFUL VOCABULARY

POINTED

ROUNDED HILLOCK

NOSE

BALD

CHAPTER 16 - 1,078 Miles!

I wake to the sound of rain and wind.

At breakfast I learn that I'm not the only one to be concerned about the sheep. The farmer comes to tell all six of us round the table that she's still poorly, but alive, and that the vet is coming shortly to move her to a shed so that she can be ill in comfort out of the rain. Her baby will stay with her, for the moment anyway. It's all rather poignant, but I am not strong enough to resolve never to eat lamb again.

After this bulletin, breakfast conversation touches on the subject of 'time'. Time it was when we didn't have clocks, calenders or diaries. There was 'task time' instead. This was before factories, of course, and paid labour. A task, like harvesting for instance, was allowed as much time as was necessary. One was unlikely to have a diary in which it was noted that harvesting could only take two days because a week on the Costa del Sol had been booked at a bargain price for the following day. This makes me think. The rain is teeming down and I don't feel like going out in it. Should I stay here for a day or two and leave when I 'feel' like it? Maybe I should not rush to complete my task/undertaking. Perhaps it's a mistake to have such a firm focus on my destination; maybe I should listen to the vibrations of the universe to guide me as to the 'right' time to complete my travels. As I inwardly contemplate a possible extension of my plans, my eyes stray through the big picture window, down the long garden to the road along which I catch sight of two, by now rather familiar figures. I'm sure it's Ine and Frits, battling against the elements. This galvanises me into action. Now there's no question of staying. How namby pamby. How weak. This is my last day of cycling, and I'm daring to procrastinate. This just won't do.

But it really is a battle against the elements. Yesterday's calm and sunny evening has changed into steady rain with an east wind. Judging from the vegetation, the prevailing wind up here is from the north, although my landlady insists it's south west. I just don't understand. But wind or no wind it's just a matter of getting to my next stop, Thurso, as steadily as possible. I have passed into Caithness, and the landscape is flatter and less dramatic than Sutherland. It does not lend itself to my habitual Tolkein-esque imaginings.

I pass the Dounreay Visitor Centre, which I would like to look round but I am too wet. I reach Thurso and am padlocking the bike to railings outside a bistro when Frits appears in the doorway, beckoning me inside. He and Ine have finished their coffee and were just about to leave, but they sit with me for a little while as I try to dry out. They too are very wet and leave shortly afterwards for their final burst to JOG. After my hot chocolate I make the mistake of routinely going to spend a penny. It is excrutiatingly unpleasant as I drag on my cold, damp knickers, damp padded pants and damp shorts. It's almost a relief to get out into the rain again and get properly wet!

On the way out of Thurso, I see a sign reading 'John O'Groats - 20'. This is *IT*, then. The very last leg. Although I really need to finish as soon as possible, I feel even more strongly that I want to savour every single remaining mile.

By the time I reach Mey the rain has stopped and I have a bowl of soup in a pub along the road. As I'm nicely drying out, I decide to pay a visit to the Queen Elizabeth the Queen Mother's Castle Mey which, in a manner of speaking, is practically next door to the pub, and which she has kindly gifted to the nation. All the same, the nation has to pay £7 per serf head to shuffle through the royal portals. We obediently keep in line on the correct side of a rope, which is slung across the doorway of each room, while super-serfs efficiently explain the provenance of the objects inside each room and how the Queen Mother spent her time in it. We respectfully bob our heads at each fascinating fact we learn of her lifestyle, and I try to think of any other woman in history who's had *two* 'Queens' in her title, and I'm not surprised when I can't, not really being very up in these matters.. There are watercolours by Prince Charles and oils by Prince Philip. It's difficult to judge who is the better painter. Although I am not a castle person, I have to admit that I would have this one. I would get rid of all the rubbish inside, but the castle itself is exquisite. Small, intimate, windows everywhere, so the rooms are flooded with light. It seems this is the only property she ever owned, and I surprise myself by thinking that the nation should be grateful that she rescued it from dereliction.

I just about manage to cycle back down the half mile drive with a cross wind without being blown off. Castle Mey is practically next door to JOG, and in no time I have arrived - in clear, chilly sunshine. I pass the sign, then turn left down to the sea where a cluster of buildings serves tourists' needs and ferries set off for the Orkneys. I feel slightly flat and wonder where Frits and Ine have got to as they were ahead of me. I have also been expecting to see Brunnhilde but presume that she decamped early as it was so wet this morning, and has probably reached the Orkneys by now, as that was her plan. I see a tandem bicycle propped up against a wall but there's no sign of its riders. But as I come out of the ferry office I am delighted to see Ine and Frits cycling towards me with big smiles on their faces and waving bunches of wild flowers, which they thrust into my hands. They say they saw me from their hotel window, took a picture of me cycling into JOG, and then jumped on their bikes to come and meet me. And then Wendy and Dan join us and it's congratulations all round. They have been all the way to Cape Wrath, which is a tremendous detour. We have a little party of photos and general rejoicing, and then Wendy and Dan leave for the hostel which is where I shall also be staying tonight. I have a last drink with Frits and Ine in the café. We agree to meet the following morning on the ferry as I want to spend a day on the Orkneys while I wait for Will to drive all the way up here to collect me.

As I cycle back towards Canisbay, the wind has shifted to the west! It's a very, very hard three miles to the hostel, real teeth-gritting stuff, and I realise that I was lucky not to have had it this strong before, which makes me wonder that perhaps it wasn't always against me, as I thought! It certainly seemed so at the time. When I arrive at the hostel, I'm presented with a Certificate for the Lands End to John O'Groats journey, which is a formality that I imagine has to be carried out most days!

That evening I browse through the stack of journals filled in with entries of End-to-End travellers' tales; punctures, people, places, etc. Nearly everybody records the sense of achievement they feel, nearly everybody describes similar feelings to mine, and it seems trite to put down more or less the same things, but what does that matter? It will take me some time to sort out what I really feel. For now I'm just happy to be here. And happy not to have to plan tomorrow's route ... or tomorrow's bed.

AFTERWORD

When I first conceived the idea of this trip, it seemed an almost impossible dream. It seemed highly unlikely to me, even while I was planning it, that I would - or could - cycle so far, on my own, doing my own navigating and decision making.

It seemed risky, and indeed quite unlikely, that I would do it at all. But at the same time, something was telling me that it wasn't a crazy idea, or at least not as crazy as crossing the Sahara on a camel, as I once dreamed of doing with little knowledge of deserts and none at all of camels.

Now, having done it, it seems like nothing at all.

It does not seem such a great achievement. It seemed a much greater one before I did it, than after! In fact, the most arduous part of the trip turned out to be writing it up! So much easier just to cycle mindlessly each day, imagining a rolled-up ribbon of road unwinding behind me.

When people learn of my ride, they ask just three questions: "Were you bored?", "Were you lonely?" and "Were you afraid?".

In answering them, I can honestly say that the challenge of constant concentration while I was on the bike meant that I was very rarely bored and the ever-changing stream of new acquaintances I met on the road combined with the busy-ness of planning left little time for loneliness.

And though I was never truly afraid, I was aware of an ever-present nagging anxiety and apprehension, usually connected with where I was staying! Either because I didn't have a clue or because I did, which meant I knew only too well how far I had to cycle to reach it.

Truth to tell, by the time I reached John O'Groats I was addicted to cycling. I could have gone on for ever. And my head, which had buzzed for years with the need to do the big something for myself, had quietened. I had known I had to do it. I had known I needed to leave my comfort zone for a while to be able to appreciate its pleasures.

I would love to do the whole trip again, but the experience could never be repeated. Next time it might be France, or maybe the Pilgrims' Way in Spain, or the North Sea Route and maybe rendezvousing with Brunnhilde or Ine and Frits, or ...

I have discovered how utterly pleasurable, and easy, it is to get away from it all, on two wheels. Most people like to stick to the main roads, venturing little into unknown territory, but with a rudimentary knowledge of map reading, you can find little bits of heaven everywhere....and if you cycle, you can hear heaven too!

Finally, I have to thank my trusty steed from the bottom of my heart. On returning home, the first trip to the supermarket led to a puncture ...

APPENDIX - Some Useful Addresses

Cyclists' Touring Club
PO Box 510
Unit 8 Fleming Way
Isleworth TW7 6WP
tel: 0870 873 0061
fax: 0870 873 0065
e-mail: membership@ctc.org.uk
web: www.ctc.org.uk

Youth Hostels Association
Trevelyan House
Dimple Road
Matlock
Derbyshire DE4 3YH
tel: 01629 592 600
fax: 01629 592 702
web: www.yha.org.uk

Scottish Youth Hostels Association
7 Glebe Crescent
Stirling FK8 2JA
tel: 01786 891 400
fax01786 891 350
web: www.syha.org.uk

Blue Hostel Guide
IBHS Secretary
PO Box 7024
Fort William PH33 6YX
Scotland
web: www.hostel-scotland.co.uk

British Waterways
Albert House
Quay Place
92/93 Edward Street
Birmingham B1 2RA
tel: 0121 200 7400

Bikewise
61 Swakeleys Road,
Ickenham, Uxbridge
Middlesex UB10 8DQ
tel: 01895 675376

Ingleborough View Guest House
Proprietors - Sue & Geoff King
Main Street
Ingleton
Carnforth LA6 3HH
tel: 01524 241 523
e-mail: stay@ingleboroughview.com

Primrose Cottage
Proprietor - Helen Jones
Orton Road
Tebay
Cumbria CA10 3TL
tel: 015396 24791
mob: 0777 852 0930
web:
www.primrosecottagecumbria.co.uk
e-mail: primrosecottebay@aol.com

Howard House
Proprietors - Lawrence & Sandra
Fisher
27 Howard Place
Carlisle
Cumbria CA1 1HR
Tel: 01228 529 159
fax: 01228 512 550
e-mail: howardhouse@bigfoot.com

Lora House
Proprietor - Margaret Gravell
Connel
Oban
Argyll PA37 1PA
Tel: 01631 710456

Solway Sporting Breaks
Proprietors - Roger & Helen Pascoe
2 Queensberry Terrace
Cummertrees,
Dumfriesshire DG12 5QF
tel: 01461 700333
web: www.solwaysportingbreaks.co.uk
e-mail: solwaysb@aol.com

Aulton Farm House
Proprietor - Agnes Hawkshaw
Aulton Farm
Kilmaurs KA3 2PQ
Kilmarnock
tel: 01563 528208

The Bed and Breakfast
Proprietors - Mandy & Lindsay Smith
1 Macleod Crescent
Altnaharra
Lairg
Sutherland IV27 4UG
tel: 01549 411258
web: www.altnaharra.net
e-mail: info@altnaharra.net

Tigh-Na-Clash Guest House
Proprietors - Ian & Joan Ritchie
81 Melvich - by Thurso
Sutherland KW14 7YJ
tel/fax: 01641 531262
web: www.tighnaclash.co.uk
e-mail: joan@tighnaclash.co.uk

Skinners Ash Farm
Proprietors – BJ & JS Godfrey
Fenny Bridges
Honiton
Devon EX14 3BH

Bro-Anneth B&B
Proprietor – Sue Williams
Leedstown
Hayle
Cornwall
01736 850 224